ARRIVAL PRESS

SOUTH EAST VOICES

1992

First published in Great Britain in 1992 by
ARRIVAL PRESS
3 Wulfric Square, Bretton,
Peterborough, PE3 8RF

Foreword

Arrival Press was formed in 1991 to promote the
writing of poetry, often previously unpublished,
from the thousands of contemporary, novice and
established poets - old and young alike.

South East 1992 reflects the intriguing and
entertaining variety of subjects poets are writing
about today.

I'm sure you will enjoy reading this anthology
as much as I have; and I hope it presents a fitting
and lasting testimony to poets throughout the
South East of the Country.

Contents

Inspiration	Douglas Armstrong	1
Rumty-Tum Poets	Alan Bignell	2
Missing the Bus	Colin Larmer	3
Feelings	A Burnett	4
Racism	Ashika Patel	5
The Civilian Amry	Elizabeth Merifield	6
'Woman's Body Found in Flat'	Sylvia Dewhirst	7
Untitled	Rebekah Smart	9
One Who is Dying of AIDS	D W Fincham	10
Terrorist	Peter Norris	11
Camping in Greece	Michael Foster	12
The End of the Day	Helen Tebbutt	13
The Changing Age	Joan Brooks	14
Urban Parting	Daniel Blythe	15
Spring Song	Rosemary Young	16
Expiation	Doreen Clark	17
To Victory and Death!	Cyril Saunders	18
Joy	Tom Buchanan	19
Life Goes On	Kay Peerless	20
Birthday Dedication	Elaine Teague	21
A Lover's Tale	Lee Dickens	22
Suicide, The Solution - But is it?	Karen Tyler	23
The Cat	Michael Bartlett	24
By the Sea	Andrew Mussell	25
Find Time for Tears	Henrietta Ross Hodgson	26
On Purchasing a Copy of the Hereford Mappa Mundi	Bill Cooper	27
Space	Dawn Fransella	28
'Trust Me'	Penny Evans	29
Birth	June Hawkins	31
My Little Winner	Jakki Wheeler	33
The Laughing Boy From Montreal	Mick Stannard	34
A Member of the Family	Steve Everest	35

Prep for the Hols	D Chedzey	36
Kaleidoscope	May Haywood	37
Thoughts on a Brass Rubbing	Winnie L Oakley	38
Rainbows	B King	39
Forbidden Love	P Tooth	40
Concrete	Anna Clements	41
Untitled	Val Greenland	42
Native From the Jungle	Tony Watson	43
At Mediobogdum	Arnold Bloomer	45
Our Son	Mary Bryant	47
Tribute to Love	Gavin Parker	48
In Memory of Darren	Anton Galea	49
Eighty Words a Minute	Linda Clarke	50
Renaissance	Claire Dannatt	51
Hurt	Tracey Cooper	52
The Big Mistake	Barbara Crouch	53
For Topaz; Two Weeks Old	Fynn Stirm	54
Stiff Upper Lip	Lynn Sanders	55
Rain	Richard Langridge	57
Green Eyes	C Small	58
Heart's Ease	Margaret Day	59
Langdon Cliff on a Sad Summer's Day	Anthony Lyng	60
Writers Peace	Margaret Marshall	62
Sharing, or All This and Heaven Too	Marjorie Kewish	63
You Are ...	Vanessa Galloway	64
Mind-Reader ...	Gary Hayes	65
Untitled	Tracie Amis	66
Sometime	E Reynolds	67
The Questioner	P Pollero	69
When We Were Young	Elsie Rodgers	71
Sorry. To a Point	Gill Moore	72
The Orient Express	John Arnold	74
Ascendio Ad Absurdam	Jock Mills	75
Stars	Yvonne Cornwall	76
Christmas Eve	Marjorie Chapman	77

Forever Seventeen	Tracy Varndell	78
Untitled	J King	79
The Divided Self	Kathy Toop	81
Inpressions in Sand	Beth Fender	82
My England	Jonathan Field	83
Time	D Rochester	84
Darkness	Mark Eaton	85
Why Don't we Care?	Anna Georgiou	86
A Question of Christmas	Elizabeth Hardy	87
Divorce	S Ford	88
On Seeing a New Baby	Barbara Hussey	89
Past Present and Future	Karen Rollins	90
Exiled by High Heels	Rasjidah St John	91
If Only	Y Bell	92
No Reason Given	Naomi-Ruth Burden	93
God's Wonderful World	Eunice C Squire	94
Anxious Days	Juliette Seagrave	95
Regrets on a Winter's Day	E Jones	96
After the Telling	J A Lock	97
Age	M Jeffery	98
Spinster Looks Back	Helen Grundy	99
Rememberings	Sybil Steel	100
Thoughts of England	V Garratt	101
I Don't Want to Get Involved	David Chapman	102
Seaside Dream	Jane Mirams	103
Walton on Thames Local Shop Keepers	Peter Brewer	104
The Old Harbour	Patricia Emery	105
The Boy in the Wheelchair	Bob Squire	106
Numb Reality	C Ottley	107
Rocks at Futami	Beth Porter	108
Reflections	Unicorn	109
Answers to the Questions (You Were Afraid to Ask)	Clive Gardner	110
Seasons of the Sea	David J Strawbridge	111
Dream	Nadine Strawbridge	112
It's You	I Hardy	113

Passing Time	Patricia Firmin	114
Amberley (South Downs)	Evelyn Holden	115
The Storm on Shakespeare Beach	D M Cook	116
Your Warmth	Trudi Dunlop	117
... And Tears Fell	Samantha Dunlop	118
Rubbish	Valerie Nadin	119
Dream Dance	Tom Chorlton	120
A Sad tale - But True	M Le Petit	121
Little Love	Natalie Andrews	122
On the Somme	Esther Barry	123
The Smoker	Evelyn Evans	124
The White Horse (Uffington)	Peter Young	125
Untitled	K Blake	126
The Baby-sitter	Hazel Edgington	127
An Easter Message	Henry Pugh	128
The Burglar	Pauline Brennan	129
Untitled	B W Pantling	130
The Library	Valerie Sparks	131
'Twas in a Monday Morning, Oh!	Linda E Bending	132
In the Dog-House	T V Newmark	134
S S Tranquillity	Pamela M Dean	135
Antipathy	Lal Mineham	136
Progress	Rosemary J Povey	137
Landscapes	Jean Mabey	138
The Bird Man	Judy Pavier Wilson	139
Castrato	Jonathan Pyke	140
Infinite Peace	Brenda Axworthy	141
A Poem of Sadness	Carolyn Bland	142
Avoid	Jane Evans	143
Sleepless Night	Margaret Fitchett	144
Air	R N Carpani	145
Nature at its Best	Jeannette Rose	146
Walking Through Moments	Sarah Hamblett	147
Much a Do	Jean Hands	148
Wisdom	Selay Hassan	149

Yorkshire Contacts	M E D Grason	150
The Forest of the Mind	Alex de Mierre	151
Windows of the Soul	Julie MacDonald	152
Christmas Eve Again	Pamela Courtney	153
Starry Night	Irene Hazell	154
Summer's Eve	Joyce Barnard	155
Geriatric Ward	M Patrick	157
O' Death	H W Walder	158
Too Generous With My Love	Alison Thirza	159
Contentment	Iris Allingham	160
In the City	Margaret Thompson	161
A Concoction of Smells	Stephanie Ames	162
Drugs	Karen Lucy Bianchi	163
The French Sensation	Hilary J Messeter	164
Starlings	W J Moore	166
Epitaph or Secret Drinker	Ted M Smith	167
Tough	Frances Ellen Woodfield-Readdie	168
Harvest	Charles Kaye	169
Airport	Susan Lafferty	170
The Aegian Isle of Rupert Brooke	Elizabeth Dove	171
Over Here	Marian Brodie	172
Perfect Love	J L Service	174
Reunion	Lynda Bailey	175
Waterwheel	Barbara Lane	176
Chiming of Bells	Kenneth Child	177
The Decline of a Village (Society?)	Patricia Bannister	178
Celandines	Margaret Clare	179
The Rock	Bernadette Geraghty	180
Friend of My Youth	Barbara Geraghty	181
The Oldest Magic	Michael Turton	182
Full Circle	Joan Newman	183
The Trees Infernal Reaching for Times Eternal Teaching	William Acciu	184
Broken Dream - Reawakening	Kathryn Ramsay	186

Intercity	Barley Dellaway	188
To the Spirit of Poetry	Maurice Cyril Ricks	189
Dreaming Reality	Kevin Spicer	190
Picaroon	Michael Webster	191
Yvonne Alone, Formerly Darling	Linda Young	192
The Third World	Ida Chaney	193
The Place	Richard Toogood	195
Old Man of the Beach	Simon Parker	196
Sanctuary	Nicola Bovell	197
January Afternoon	Rosemary Osborne	198
Chinese Inspiration	Ellinor Gordon Lennox	199
A Dream for All Seasons	Edward Thackeray	200
Everybody's Lovely When They Smile	Jackie Figg	201
Past and Present	Jane L Dards	202
M25	Adrian Caradine	203
Ethna: 1938-1977	Carole T O'Driscoll	204
The Last Wolf	Diana Dykes	205
The Country Lane	Jeanette Marmion	206
Track Marks	Ken Jones	207
The Bread Queue	Margery Horwood	208
The Morning Horse	D J Davies	209
Ant	Adele Misselbrook	210
Untitled	Chris Turner	211
The Carousel	Mollie Mose	212
Christmas 1987	Tony Ward	214
On Iping Bridge	Alec Annand	215
At the Moment	Carol M Harris	216
The Lonely One	L Webb	217
For Worse	Stephen Jones	218
Sea-saw	Norrie Thornton	219
Nag Nag Nag!	M Collins	220
What has he Done?	Emma Perkins	221
Dawn Above Bough Beach	Pam Hatcher	222
Who's Who in Rhyme	Dave Murphy	223
The Fight	Tracey Johnston	225

Weekend	Ruth Ellacot	226
The Harbour	Jo Appleyard	227
Horatio	Maurice West	228
The Sussex Downs	E Knight	229
In a Nutshell	Simon Baldock	230

Inspiration

Here the young heads droop.
Cramped fingers crab the cramping page:
Pens hesitate, surge on and loop.
Timed essay: Youth and Age.

Pens hesitate, surge on and loop.
Timed essay: Youth and Age.
Spirits flag and shoulders stoop
In this examination cage.

Spirits flag and shoulders stoop
In this examination cage.
Not wild-fowl in a prison-coop
Is victim to such silent rage.

Not wild-fowl in a prison-coop
Is victim to such silent rage.
Yet young minds soar and swoop
Lifting weightless in a swift rampage.

Douglas Armstrong

Rumty-Tum Poets

Your rumty-tum poet
With rinky-dink rhymes
Has little to say
Of his life and his times;

No Delphic divine, he;
No sayer of sooths;
No delver for Destiny's
Undying truths.

His soul is unbared
And he's loth to believe
He need haunt his market-place,
Heart upon sleeve.

The fancies that fly
From his Pandoric pen
Disdain the great themes
That confound other men.

He picks his way through
The world's troubles and strife
And harvests his verse
From the flip side of life.

He writes of the kitchen -
The workshop - the loo;
Lampooning the odd things
The rest of us do.

But - honestly now! -
Don't you yearn, just sometimes,
For more rumpty-tum poets
And rinky-dink rhymes?
Alan Bignell

Missing the Bus

In pain she tried, but could not hurry more,
frustrated, missed the midday twenty-four
carrying it's cargo of complacent faces,
rushing them off to destined places.

Was she alone? but no,
another equally as slow
approached; quite unobtrusively
and smiled with understanding sympathy.

Nights drawing in - changeable weather,
small talk at first as they stood together.
Could casual conversation plant a seed?,
flower in friendship, fulfil a need.

Then touching hands, togetherness,
by sharing pain, could it be less?
The timetable, faded, peeling from it's board,
mute, informative, now totally ignored.

Forgotten the painfully jolting bus,
Forgotten 'God why me', 'why us'

Colin Larmer

Feelings

Does no one have emotions now,
Or feelings any more
Affection shown goes a long, long way
To make life not a bore.

Should one not cry when one is hurt
Nor shout when one is angry
But keep within these feelings mute
And makes one ill and tawdry

Calmness I know is good for one,
And so is peace of mind
But happiness is best of all
So therefore please be kind.

A Burnett

4

Racism

Racism is one of those things,
you better watch out before you get clinged,
as you know a man was beaten,
by five white policeman.

Your not doing good picking on each other
make peace and be my brother,
I'm black and your white
What's the point of a fight.

Windows smashed fires started,
the whole wide world was tormented.
Wondering what will happen next,
everyone glued to their TV sets.

It was bad and very tragic,
I wish there was a great deal of magic,
Love ones gone people dying,
Saving their families killing or fighting.

Flames turned high and sharp,
and people killed dragged out of cars.
Innocent people defended themselves,
Carrying weapons and killing at will.

Some day things will be right
When people stop not to fight
this was because of Racism
that, that man was beaten up

Soon we will all be equal.
When no one will treat us different,
that time was a real state
and people around us still show hate.
Ashika Patel (13)

The Civilian Army

From layman came the soldier boy, sent out with gun to fight.
Dressed up in khaki uniform to wear both day and night.
The horrors of a civy-man became the normal sight.
Butcher of a different kind had turned his back on white.
When bullet flew into his breast an army man he died,
Carried to an army grave, now 'In Memorial' he lies.

At home the child and woman fought, to help to win the war.
Their back was broke' from sweat and toil, to even out the score.
They went without for country's sake, they never asked for more.
Instead they made the guns which went straight to the devil's door.
The scattered rubble of the streets, 'round bodies people cried.
The ones who never made the front were hit at home and died.

Together a country fought a war, every man, every woman and child,
With conviction that would never cease until victory, in words, was
tiled.
Yet the cost was clear for all to see, for woman and child much
sorrowed,
And also for the civy-man in the khaki suit he borrowed.

Elizabeth Merifield

6

'Woman's Body Found in Flat'

Found 'some days later,'
Lone death, pensioner
Asprawl a threadbare rug
Surrounded by cat mess, -
(Kitty being shut in with the corpse you understand).

Who would have thought it
In the years of laughter and power
When husband and children were netted
In your love and every hour
Turned to some glad purpose?

What tragedy dissolved away
The confident mature years -
Secured in ties of blood
And life assurance?

Of course she knew death waited - some time or never.
(Don't we all?)
But where's the dignity we were promised,
The solemn leave-taking,
The grandchildren's adieus?

Silver-haired old lady,
Dear old dear,
Found in filth, -
Your solitary fate appals.

Memento mori.
Sure, death visits all
And I'll refrain
From labouring such well-honed themes,
(But also pray
That kith and kindly ritual
Precede *my* pall).

Sylvia Dewhirst

Untitled

The waves run towards the beach,
Swollen bellies travelling,
The sand, whitened as with bleach,
Makes them die in a climax.
A wild crescendo of sound,
The frothing foam is released,
It bubbles across the ground,
Leaving tracks on golden sand.
The mighty waves break on rock,
Reaching height, thrown by the wind,
There are seagulls in a flock
Drowning noise with their wild cries.
The strong wind tosses all.
The salty sea spray splatters,
Crystal water droplets fall
Upon the shells and seaweed;
All cast along with the tide
Beating constantly one way.
It breaks against the cliff side,
Such a soothing violent noise.

Rebekah Smart

9

One Who is Dying of AIDS

A hooded figure in a cloak as dark
as death broods and hovers before my day
begins, as if a lover's curse should mark
my pleasure with a glance of dull dismay.
Suddenly, I sense the faint smell of stale
sweat steal suspiciously across the dawn,
for the taste of fear, prowling on the pale
and silent earth, portends a time to mourn.

A slow, wasting degeneration proves
that I won't last forever: blood and bones,
aching to the core of my body, strain,
as if to break my breath, and death removes
my feeble hold, because my life declines
to crumble to the dust where I began.

D W Fincham

10

Terrorist

My desires are sacred
No one must object
All people must bow before me
Show me great respect
What they want it does not count
Their lives are but a pawn
For I must set about my task
The reason I was born
Many children cry in pain
Why should I give a damn
For I'm a terrorist they say
A very much feared man
I will take your husbands
I will take your wifes
I will take your children too
Their innocent young lives
For all must bow before me
And do just as I say
For I will not be satisfied
Until I rule the day
And even then I may not care
Or have a thought to give
For which of you may have to die
And which of you will live.

Peter Norris

Camping in Greece

Under the olive trees
Ten nations mingle,
Share toilets and ablutions,
Swap experiences;
No common language
But unspoken thoughts
Of friendly co-existence.
Three bikers set up camp
Beside flash motor caravans.
A hitcher stumbles in
And pitches tiny tent
Next to palatial family encampment.
Night 'silence time', not heeded everywhere,
Is here obeyed implicitly, unforced.
And over all the olive branches stir,
Politically neutral, shading equally
The rich, the poor, the stronger and the weak...

Michael Foster

The End of the Day

The sky overflows; cool, deep waters,
Full of dust and old pennies,
Flowing for ever.
Eyes like brown wells, a mind softly seeping
Through to foreign lands and voids,
Tainted with crimson.

Tired of chasing old dreams,
Tired of wasting days,
Just asking yourself why,
But then you fall into the valley, her sleep once left behind,
Silenced by life's lullaby.

The walls of the room ripple and bulge,
Burnt to ashes and scattered,
Petals in the summer breeze.
The pictures now repaint themselves,
Running with hideous hues,
Flames flicker, rocked and cradled,
In nest of lavender.

Light in the distance, fire in my eyes,
No proof but the words on this page,
Not a day passes by without dreaming,
Dreaming of living to belong.

Tired of waking mornings,
Tired of listening hard
To people asking why,
Just let yourself fall into the valley of sleep and become
Silenced by life's lullaby.

Helen Tebbutt

The Changing Age

Mum would vamp on the old piano
Dad would play his violin
Willie on his mouth organ
Sis with comb and paper
Hymns on Sundays, all other days
Our favourite songs we'd sing
In fields and lanes, devoid of fear
We would gaily caper
Willie had his iron hoop
It was a noisy trick
I followed him behind
With a wooden one and stick
Hopscotch, marbles, conkers
All were our delight
With holler, squeak and whistle
In the summer twilight
Our games were so much fun
At very little cost
However times have changed
Much innocence is lost
All games and toys have
Become so very technical
In terms of money and production
They are astronomical
With music centres, calculators
On space invaders they let rip
Now it seems their lives are governed
By the expensive micro chip.

Joan Brooks

Urban Parting

The town
Was crisply winter and the sky devoured
The lemon sun. Distance was down the streets
To the brooding gasometer
And up to the frowning church.

The people, driving or walking, looked so sad,
Breath icing.

We had our junk-lunch in the frosted park
Where pigeons shivered plumply. Afterwards
We sank into a shop-womb; lights and books
And families and cards, with records that
We laughed at, near the back.
Then brittle promises were made, with eyes
And lips.

The streets are darker now, and snow
Begins to flake the glitzy fakes of shops.
The blind busker sees more than we do.

The streets are dark. The silent screams
Of lights escaping to surburbia -

The streets are dark. The empty rush of feet -

The streets so dark, and hands

Unclasping

Gone.

Daniel Blythe

15

Spring Song
(Memories of 1940)

This song recalls a distant spring,
Wild primroses and daffodils,
Our visits to your parent's home
Near woodlands, on the Sussex hills,
The chalets, promenade, the beach,
The lone expanse of sky and sea,
Sandstone cliffs, martello towers,
The castle ruins at Pevensey.

The air raid sirens drowned the calls
Of gull, scalloped above the shore,
The desolate coast, barbed-wired, sand-bagged,
Was a grim reality of the war,
Junkers chugged above the clouds,
The guns were set, no bells were rung*
And yet, to us, those days were sweet,
For it was Spring and we were young.

* Church bells were only to be rung in case of invasion, during
  World War Two.

Rosemary Young

Expiation

The young men smile from silver frames
tarnished with age.
Visored caps worn low
On beardless faces
lend a jaunty air to posed solemnity.
Greatcoat collars over exposed tender necks -
Vulnerable as early buds.
Their faces, guilless as novice nuns,
smile gently, unafraid,
their sins, if any
committed through confusion,
ours, like tumble-weed
gather momentum by the hour.

Unknowingness proved their Achilles heel -
dying mud choked in alien fields
passing through more doors than we,
who dust bloomed glass
and mounted medals in boxes,
and pin fabric poppies once a year
on Sunday suits
Flinching from the knowledge
that expiation is a privilege for the brave

Doreen Clark

17

To Victory and Death!

Where stands he now child of our youth
Sun dappled clouds have sped away
The tears that fell that summer day
When suffering had claimed its own
And nature softened changes to frown
Was it for this that yester-year
The mask of love that moved to tear
For was he not the child that seemed
So strongly felt in Mary's dream
A youth so tall, so young, so brave
One who set forth to fight, to save
The guns fall quiet, smoke fades away
And yet this thing is here to stay
He sees it not, he just plods forth
To prove to her his manhood's worth
The shell that struck him for to say
Was it then, just yesterday
When, boyhood gone and man begun
Agony masked to aid lifes plan
White sheets had cloaked his body frail
E'en when his heart began to fail
He clung to her, his mother dear
She, she alone held back the fear
That led him to a wider path
Away from war's grim angry wrath
At last he stood, a youth no more
His mind shaped so long before
And Mary now beside him stands
Flood tears held back in eager hands
All sorrow gone-he lives no more.

Cyril Saunders

Joy

Oh the joy of a broad fairway,
a long straight drive right off the tee,
The second shot on the green to stay,
and one putt for a birdie three.

Tom Buchanan

Life Goes On

The wind blows
The trees sway,
The hours drift,
So far away.
The birds sing,
The music plays,
The voices speak,
For days and days,
But...

No-ones there,
To comfort you,
No-ones there,
To see you through,
Life goes on.

The sun shines strong,
The light shines bright,
The birds all fly,
Into the night,
The tears still flow,
The pain still aches,
The wound will heal,
Loves all it takes,
But...

No-ones there,
To comfort you,
No-ones there,
To see you through,
Life goes on.

Kay Peerless

Birthday Dedication

Must listen to the radio
Today is my birthday
Hubbie's sent in a request
Wonder what they'll play.

Wonder what he's asked for
A love song I'll be bound
He can get quite romantic
He's good to have around.

I hear the DJ talking
My name I hear him say
Your Hubby thinks you're wonderful
I'll tell you if I may.

To the best home cleaning, pet feeding,
baby changing, carpet cleaning,
garden clearing, fish breeding,
table wiping, cooker cleaning, exotic dishing,
potato mashing, chip frying,
steak beating, window washing,
rose pruning, quick drying shirt ironing,
shed clearing, bed making, bath running,
toothpaste supplying, matchbox losing,
fag supplying, hard working, bacardi drinking,
wife in the world,
I love you.

Not quite what I expected
But now I know for sure
He's realised my qualities
He knows what I'm here for,

Elaine Teague

21

A Lover's Tale

You took me to the places,
- that no-ones ever been,
you filled my mind with visions,
- with you I lived my dreams.

Dancing through cornfields on tiptoe,
- barefoot through golden-soaked sands,
living as loves re-creation,
- floating through lifes-strong demands.

I stare at your picture beside me,
- and long to be there by your side,
two people in love, slightly parted,
- with a sadness they just cannot hide...

Your smiling face once filled with warmthness,
- a face that is now filled with pain,
the tears that I shed leave me broken,
- could you ever love me again?

Lee Dickins

Suicide, The Solution - But is it?

The death of a man I loved came so unexpected to me
Scott Anthony Pine was his name and an idol to me.
I loved so much this talented man
But for me he was out of reach
I was only a friend but that was good enough for me.
Time was passing but not without problems,
Inside Scott they burrowed deep
Taking everything from him, including his sanity
Eventually things just got too much
The pressure, it wouldn't go
So much he couldn't cope and decided to go
That night down the pub, I wasn't there
When Scott was saying goodbye
If I had been could I have, maybe recognised the signs.
It is a question that will never be answered
For now it's too late
My talented friend, the man I loved, is dead,
He drove out early morning of February 16th 1991
To the grounds where he once worked
Having avoided all security, Scott broke inside
Rigging up a rope, he took his own life.
Coming to terms with Scott's death
it was so very hard for me
I couldn't believe someone like him could do such a thing to me,
So much sorrow, pain and heartache
It is what death leaves behind
So to all you people out there
No matter how bad things may seem
Someone will always be loving you
Please don't shatter life's dream.

(Dedicated to Scott A Pine)

Karen Tyler

The Cat

Along the fence stalks the cat
Soft, sleek and black
Tease the German Shepherd on the right
And the Jack Russell, out of sight
The fence wobbles
Yet she never topples
Ruler of this patch
A beast that none can match

Michael Bartlett (15)

By the Sea

Have you seen the spectacle of England by the sea
The people upon the promenade
The seagulls flying free

Fish and chips and candy floss vanish by the tons
The kids are laughing, sleeping, fighting
But generally having fun

Tired old mares in striped deck chairs dream of days gone by
Walking hand in hand along the sand
Their best man by their side

Brightly coloured souvenir shops with their wares for all to see
Buckets and spades and rubber rings
And hats that say, 'Kiss me'

The stony beach is empty now but the waves keep rolling in
The stony beach is empty
Save the plastic and the tins

Andrew Mussell

Find Time for Tears

When love dies,
And the once bright light in her eyes
Has faded like fallen petals on the grass,
And you feel trapped in a morass
Of mixed emotions and real fears,
Find time for tears,
And let your grieving heart
Obtain relief; for tears are part
Of the blessed healing balm.

Tears are the drops that ease the pain;
After a hot spell as welcome as the rain
Upon the flowers and the parched lawn.
Then, after she has gone,
Stand quietly aside, take stock and think,
You may be standing on the brink
Of some fresh delight.
And sure as day will follow night,
A new beginning and a sweet calm.

Henrietta Ross Hodgson

On Purchasing a Copy of the Hereford Mappa Mundi

Upon my wall there hangs a map, a medieval chart,
That shows the world as it once was in every detailed part,
Some seven hundred years ago it was when it was drawn,
When our modern scientific sense had not as yet been born,
Copernicus had not yet held that earth goes round the sun,
Nor Newton come with gravitas nor Leonardo's gun,
Nor Galileo's telescope nor Stephenson's hot steam,
Nor any man of science who has entertained the dream,
Of raising man above the gods to become supremely wise,
To eat the fruit of knowledge that would open up the eyes,
That every single one of us should view himself divine,
And with measuring rods and compasses the universe define,
My map was drawn in better days when earth was undefiled,
With industrial pollutants and its politics so wild,
The earth was green and all the world lived in a Golden Age,
Where disease and poverty went unchecked and bubonic plague did
rage,
Where they who ranged beyond the bounds of official thought did
make,
That terrifying journey from the dungeon to the stake,
Where babies died in infancy and infidels were slain,
In their thousands by crusading knights who were blessed by church
profane,
Ah, if only we could have the best of both these worlds, my Lord,
Where pruning-hooks are made from spears and plough-shares from
the sword,
Where fields are green and water pure, where innocence is cherished,
Where for once it is the good who bloom and evil men who perish,
Where every man with thanks does find his place in Your creation,
Where the kingdoms all belong to You with all the world one nation,
Would such a world be possible? Could we draw it on a map?
Or make of it a little book that rests upon our lap?
Or a larger tome all leather bound that sits on library shelves?
Thy Kingdom come, Thou Blessed One, and save us from ourselves!
Bill Cooper

Space

Space?   What is space?
A void filled with stars,
Planets,
Meteorites,
Galaxies,
Infinite space,
Receding galaxies,
Receding where too?
Humans on a planet,
But a speck of dust,
If Earth is receding,
what of us.

Dawn Fransella

'Trust Me'

'I'm going to Doncaster tonight,
I have to see my old friend Joe,
Look darling, I've told you ten times,
and the answer must still be no.

No. You can't come with me love,
Now please don't look at me that way,
Joe would never understand it,
And I wouldn't know what to say.

Now darling I know you've never met him,
But I promise one day you will,
I'm only going for one day,
And yes, of course I love you still.

Darling I'll be back on Wednesday,
Now you be good while I'm away,
I'm only going to Leeds dear
No Doncaster I meant to say"

And so I see you to the door,
I smile and I kiss you goodbye,
You're going away without me,
And inside I still wonder why.

Maybe Joe's short for Joesephine?
Perhaps Doncaster's really Leeds?
Is there someone who can better,
Satisfy your desires and needs?

I tell myself I'm being silly,
Our love is far too strong a link,
I know no one could take my place,
Yes I really trust you --- I think.

Penny Evans

Birth

Lying exhausted on the bed
Beads of sweat running down my head
Lie still I think, it's not too bad
In a little while, he could be a dad
Here it comes again the rush of pain
Oh god do all women feel the same?
And just when I think you can take no more
A cheerful face looks round the door
All right dear? the nurse calls out
No it's not, I want to shout
But I whisper, 'I could do with a drink'
'Back in a minute', She says
What the hell I think
I didn't want her brisk reply
I'm all alone again, and want to cry.

Why doesn't someone come I'm bursting to go
I ring the bell and hear someone cry oh
I didn't scream it wasn't me
Oh why can't they just let me be?
Pulling me this way and that
Nurse says 'Just roll on your side' and gives me a pat
'We're nearly there' She says with a smile
'When I say push push hard all the while'
I feel as though I am tearing in two
'Hold it' She cries 'The head's now in view
try panting a bit, that's it dear
The head's nearly out, good the shoulders are here

Now give all you've got and push down hard'
The words I thought then would have sure got me barred
I must have dozed off, when I heard a shrill scream
Then the nurse was saying 'Hold up dear we must have him clean'
I opened my eyes and looked, to where the voice had come
And there was the nurse, holding my new born son

June Hawkins

My Little Winner

With a soaking wet nappy
And tired eyes,
He stands in his cot in a temper
And cries.

He screams at breakfast
And louder at lunch,
Then throws his toys till they break
with a crunch.

When Daddy comes home
He squeals with delight,
Then chases the cat who runs off
In a fright.

He lays in his cot at seven
After dinner,
Then drifts quietly to sleep
My little winner.

(To Alex and James)

Jakki Wheeler

33

The Laughing Boy From Montreal

I still recall the softest kiss
that touched my lips as frozen ice.
And held me close beside your breath
 a freshly blooded sacrifice.
Yet shrouded in the splintered rain
of sunlight through the curtains drawn,
awakened from the sweetest dream
to find a sadness newly born.

And crawling 'neath the barrier
that lead along the midnight path,
my broken heart began to melt
and wash away your photograph.
Once more the face of emptiness
lay staring at these barren walls.
And I was left alone to fight
the Laughing Boy from Montreal.

Mick Stannard

A Member of the Family

The timid start and quiv'ring fright,
Teaching the young one wrong from right,
The first deft slap, the howling night,
The first day out, the first lost fight.

The calming down, accustomed place,
Of howling youth there is no trace,
An upright citizen contented prowls,
Setting daily, gentle, relaxed pace.

Then dribbling starts, the loss of hair,
A greyness round the wrinkling face,
The pace slows down, the sight impaired,
A fireside is his hiding place.

The days and months crawl slowly past,
The ingrown cancer gnaws its last,
A last quiet stroke from kindly vet,
Is haunting memory of a love-drenched pet.

Steve Everest

Prep for the Hols

How was your day at the office? Mine was not so good.
Your Mother phoned at half past nine, like I said she would.
It seems she's had another turn, similar to last year,
As soon as we're going on holiday, she starts to shed her tears.
My shopping trolley wheel came off, can you fix it with a screw?
I've got all the camping grub to buy, and I've got a list for you.
Collect the travel sickness pills, some flea spray for the dog.
Then get a battery for the torch in case we hit some fog.
The electric bill arrived today, a hundred and twenty two;
Better pay it while you're out, we don't want it overdue.
Young Jimmy needs new trainers, I wish he wouldn't climb,
Oh the baby has a funny rash, so get some calamine.
I've put your case out on the bed, lay out what you're taking my dear,
And don't forget your underpants like you did last year.
Tomorrow lunchtime, take the key round to Mrs Gower's.
She'll feed the cats and check the house and, water all your flowers.
What's that you said? You're planning what?
A morning's golf with friends?
Unless you want a quick divorce - here's where your planning ends.

D Chedzey

Kaleidoscope

What is this grey shadow that keeps stalking me?
It sneaks up behind, I'm never quite free.
It is named pain I'm forced to admit,
I try to fight it, I walk, talk and sit.
But the grey shadow will still come and go.
I now dread the nights, their passing so slow.
The waves that get stronger as my will gets weak,
There's no escaping it, solace I seek.
The moment has come, grey shadow has gone
But in its place is the black face of pain,
Relentless it stands there, I know defeat
Others must nurse me, my surrender complete.
Now all is redness, I lie here inert
The shock of the knife, the weakness, the hurt.
How can this body ever feel mine?
White caps and aprons, white beds in line,
Bandages, draining tubes, whiteness abounds,
Surgical white coats proceed on their rounds.
One day I notice the flowers by my bed,
Pink cheeks of the nurses, lips cherry red.
I start to taste food, brown gravy, gold fish.
Cards from my friends, 'Every good wish.'
Then the day comes when I walk to the door,
Blue sky overhead, green fields before.
Buttercups, dandelions, daisies so white,
I raise my head and see God's golden light.

May Haywood

37

Thoughts on a Brass Rubbing

Stately and still
In your gown of lace,
I ponder and gaze
On your silent face.
What was your life?
Was it good or bad?
What were your thoughts?
Were they happy or sad?
Did you love? Did you hate?
What was your fate?
Yours are these secrets
Locked in the stone,
Mine is your beauty,
That alone.

Winnie L Oakley

Rainbows

Misty morning, dark grey cloud
Wispy willow hid by a shroud
I looked skyward as noon approached

A myriad refraction
I saw above
Multi-colour refraction
For you, my love

Red for the setting sun
Orange for the winter sun
Yellow for the golden sand
Green, the leaves of summer
Blue, the colour of your eyes,
Of clear summer skies
Indigo and violet
The colours of night

All combined in a spinning wheel
A white of whites they do reveal
White so pure, white so bright

White, the colour of the snow
The carpet of snow
Covering all in winter
Covering my mind,
Thinking of rainbows

B King

39

Forbidden Love

No arms to fold around me, no comfort and no word
No love to get lost in, my loneliness goes unheard
What happened in my darkest time, my hour of despair
I turned around to look for you but you were not there
I needed someone to cling to, a very special friend
Of trust and understanding, a shoulder for to lend
My life was torn in pieces there was nothing left to tear
But when I turned to look for you, you *wasn't* even there
I needed someone beside me to make my life worthwhile
To comfort and protect me, to make me want to smile
I wanted you more than all the World but knew that was unfair
Because every time I turned for you, I searched but you weren't there
Your life belongs to you and that's the way it has to be
Although you need someone too that someone isn't me
To feel the love I feel for you is *something* very rare
But I'll no longer turn for you for you never will be there
Now in my grief I thank you for the way you were with me
Although I always knew, you never would be free
I know now only one thing in my heart I'll always care
And if by chance you turn for me I always will be there

P Tooth

Concrete

She falls down hard,
Slap, on the concrete.
It's not the first time.
Beer can in hand,
Smile on his evil face.
He kicks her, makes her get up,
She holds her head as he yells at her.
The damage done to her body is nothing compared
to the scars left on her heart.

Anna Clements (13)

41

Untitled

Why is there no silver lining?
In this troubled world I see.
Why is there no love nor human contact?
Just war in every territory.
No one sees the sun shining,
No one sees the birds and trees,
Only hopelessness and desecration.
This surely was not *meant* to be!
How can I turn the corner?
Find a green and pleasant land,
Turn to joy instead of sorrow,
Knowing love is close a hand,
Who will help me find peace?

Val Greenland

Native From the Jungle

I was deep in the jungle
Early one morning
Seeing to my breakfast
That I never had

No corner shop or local band
Just swamp's and sinking sand
No pet puppy dog's or fluffy duck's
Just massive great tiger's and slimy green crocks

Something made me jump
And I turned around
I thought it was a native

I offered him breakfast
But he didn't except
He pulled out his knife
So I said 'Here's dinner instead'

No corner shop or local band
Just swamp's and sinking sand
No Pet puppy dog's or fluffy duck's
Just massive great tiger's and slimy green crocks

I swung in the jungle from tree to tree
Then something made me jump
And I turned around
It was an ugly great ape chasing me

I am a hero and a marvellous man
'cos I came back with the Quinkakclan
Just take my word
And make this heard
Never go to the jungle
Unless you're a squered.

Tony Watson

At Mediobogdum

Flamboyant fortress, elevated high,
commanding camp site, backed by scree impregnable.
The Romans built it to protect their western flank,
where now rise up the fuming towers of Sellafield.

Played here the bawdy soldiery,
lascivious glances at the virgin bint
in Eskdale's green below, conjecturing.

Strode here the haughty legionaries,
transplanted from their native, sun-baked soil.
No week-end passes to the streets of Rome,
no annual leave in Naples or Turin -
just binding boredom in the garrison.
The glory? Active service - *overseas!*

This annexation of a foreign land
contrived a marriage of two disparate cultures.
In time the foothold weakened;
new victory potential was the bait
to lure away the military machine
and leave the children fatherless.

Gone the grip of alien tyranny. Now the ruins
give way to ruined ruins,
beautiful in cherished preservation.

Another marriage hovers in the west,
not culture-based, but borne upon the wind.
This time there'll be no lust, no tears
at parting from some dark-skinned mystery man
who speaks a foreign tongue and loves with passion.
Only cloud, invisible germs and dust - that spell
a sure destruction in our marrow,
not even ruined ruins, and no tomorrow.

Arnold Bloomer

Our Son

O Perry what we gave to you,
Was the world so bright and new,
Thunderstorms, rain, wind and sun,
You are still our number one.

You brought us so much fun and laughter,
We thought it would last forever after,
But now you have gone up to the sky,
With the angels to guard you, you know why.

So blessed little one of ours,
We will always bring you flowers,
Every day we will always think of you,
Knowing you will be thinking of us too.

With warm affections you would show,
You could tell we love you so,
With the clouds soaring high,
Now we have to say goodbye.

We will always carry the pain,
For we will never see you again,
But with the memories we will treasure,
Never to forget them for ever.

Mary Bryant

Tribute to Love

Love is a beautiful thing.
It can send the soul to dizzying heights of ecstasy
and without it the soul can become a dead thing.
The love of woman for man and man for woman is the search of
many,
but many find only purgatory.
Give me your love O beautiful woman, let me take you to a place
where we can be alone and free, just you and me.
Where the insane hatred of those who kindle hate mean nothing
and cannot touch us.
Just us my love and love, for all eternity and ever after.

Gavin Parker

In Memory of Darren

A theatrical sparkle,
Shines from a young face,
With sparkling blue eyes,
Looking at the world,
Set in a pace.
Companion brother friend,
Gelled with a humour,
No one heard a sound
On that November day,
Of his last life murmur,
As his life passed away.
A mechanical lift,
Dangerous to one,
Over-ridden by a switch,
Supervised by none.
Pulled up by supportive hands,
By the gracious one God.
Introducing to his spirit,
To become, again one.
Time now in heaven.
He looks on us all.
Being part of our lives,
Being part of us all.
Fond memories and thoughts
Floating through our minds,
His friends, family people,
Wishing he was here,
Darren, so dear.

Anton Galea

Eighty Words a Minute

It was February and the wind was bitter, the municipal park
empty apart from us, who'd come to honour
Cynthia's redundancy.
I've got my skills, was all she had to say,
eighty words a minute, girls, they can't take those away.

*It's not the end of the world,*she said.
So we slopped the wine into the paper cups
and toasted the world not having ended, quite,
and the cold wind blew away
the perfume she always called *Anay Anay.*
Those long nails curled around her cigarette,
those narrowed eyes, that mouth made smaller still
to drag the smoke inside, red painted, red on red.
She clattered up and down on spiked heels
and every now and then she'd pause to stare
hard down into the patent leather
as if to read the future clearer there.

She's got her skills, they can't take those away.
They'll take your face and your fertility,
the bloom of youth, your sexuality,
your hope, your laughter and your dignity,
but eighty words a minute - no, they won't take those away.

Linda Clarke

50

Renaissance

A shell, strong and empty.
A form created by others, moulded by convention,
Expectation and a striving to be perfect, to please.
Inside something stirs, an embryonic form
That has lain silent longing for recognition.
She is weak and not yet fully formed. In part
She wants to break the shell and be free
But it is too soon., The form is too vulnerable,
Too uncertain. She needs to grow and develop inside
Before she can take flight. This nucleus
Can shed the layers of her shell bit by bit
As she grows, and slowly let go of the known
And step into the unknown.
She can discard the masks and roles employed to
Please and remain safe.
The embryo can learn to believe in herself,
Trust her thoughts and actions
And follow her intuition.
She will grow and one day be able to peel off
The final layer of the shell and see the world
Through her own eyes, not someone elses.
To find her own identity and celebrate
The birth of her selfhood.

Claire Dannatt

Hurt

It comes and goes, nobody knows
exactly where it comes from

Hiding anxious to pounce on it's prey.
Attacking the tender part of one
man's heart.

He's adoration and devotion is
torn into shreds, his love isn't
enough.

Mind and body become a farrago,
everything caves in,
and decomposes, his feelings
have inefficiency to react.

Changes take place,
the exterior looks as bad as the
internal.

Damaged his body shouts for attention,
the need for help.
Though little he knows, all will.

Tracey Cooper

The Big Mistake

A strange man built a strange building
And people thought him a fool
He said he had done it for the children
And he went and named it *School*.

He invented the school bell
He invented school time,
He invented school dinners
And I think that was a crime.

He invented school papers,
He invented school books,
He invented school pencils,
And He invented school looks.

He invented school playgrounds,
He invented school gates,
He invented school assembly,
He even invented mistakes.

So life goes by and we all make mistakes,
As too did this strange creature,
Do you know the biggest mistake he ever did make?
He went and invented the teacher.

Barbara Crouch

53

For Topaz; Two Weeks Old

Whence come the hands
that shake the tree
and the apples are words
and the words are me

it's the wind, my son
who strokes your heart's cheek
it's the wind
who caresses your industrious day
with a gentle tune
from his scented loom

and the apples that fall
are no tears but a vow
and the vow bears the fruit
and the tree bows its crown

and the crown
is the smile in the eyes of the blessing
touching the tree
that is me

Fynn Stirm

Stiff Upper Lip

I'm down from't North, just to explore
and meet me future Mum-In-Law.
I've just arrived in me best frock,
Experiencing Culture Shock!

We've left Aunt Flo asleep in't chair
While we go off and let down hair -
A shopping trip has been suggested,
Now Auntie's fed, all food digested.

The car's installed in't Multi-Storey
So off we set in all our glory
Shops' treasure trove at our disposal
To celebrate our new betrothal.

All plastic bags and aching feet
We have a pre-set time to meet.
The car-park is our rendezvous -
We must return - Flo's tea is due.

On our return, there sits Aunt Flo,
False teeth adrift, skin ashen glow.
The dog has rumbled summat's up,
While Mum brews up a cheering cup.

How am I going to break the news?
I'll have a think while the tea brews.
Still, I suppose it's nice to know
There must be much worse ways to go.

The Doctor's called, he's on his way,
There's really nothing one can say
So cup in hand we have a sit
And toast Aunt Flo's stiff upper lip.

Lynn Sanders

Rain

I was desert. Personality in a dust bowl
My achievements withered in an arid soil.
Dreams like twisted stalks
Scattered on a sloping ground
A conscience made of broken stones
A barren mind on which an angry sun refused to set.
This was the landscape of my soul
Until you came.
You were the rain.
At first only a whisper on the wind
A missed beat in the morning's song
I did not think you would
So softly lay down moisture
Along the contours of my heart,
While I was facing the other way.
Then, few moments left before the arid plain
I turned, and found my life in flower.
I need you still
And ever greater wells to hold you in.
My climate's changed
My soul is spring
I am green meadow now
Come, lay yourself on me.

Richard Langridge

Green Eyes

Greenly glowing pools,
Relentless dangerous tools.
Experienced use of which
E'er causes hearts to twitch.
Nothing quite so sure
Every man wants more,
Yet they know that they
Every time must pay,
Since she does nought but play!

C Small

58

Heart's Ease

I go into the countryside to fill my heart
Which in the town is but an empty cup.
I walk the hills and lanes in sun and shadow
Drinking my fill of natures' healing wine.

The solitude of slumbrous summer days
When leaves weave canopies against the sun
To make of woods a dappled sanctuary,
A darkened well of softly falling silence.

To walk in stubbled fields in Autumn's season
To see birds rise into a violet sky.
Feel little breezes, speaking soft of winter's coming
And tread a leaf-made carpet's russet pile.

Margaret Day

Langdon Cliff on a Sad Summer's Day

The jostling juggernauts bustled noisily
into the bowels of a streamlined slash
of coloured Logos euphemistically called a ship
but in reality little more than a megalithic box
floating on the oil-smooth sea in the womb-shaped harbour.

A sky lark and then a thrush vainly tried to compete
with loud discordant diesel noise
as white flecks of angry foam protested in the open sea.

The anxious, strained faces of those
patiently hoping to ease their packet of joy onto the RORO
shone out through the industrial tangle of the port
whilst a small lobster boat harmoniously rode the disquiet waters.

A white sail and billowing spinaker
was a palimpsest of things that used to be.

People walked hand in hand through the thorn bushes on
the tranquil cliff top - using their imagination
to transcend the noise and smoked veils
into nature's peace and freedom.
Honeysuckle lent its fragrance to their brief idyll
of sanguine blissfulness.

The slight chill of the sea breeze lofting gulls and terns helped
my escape to contemplation of the joys of natural freedom.

The shadow of my reality cut across these levitating thoughts
as did the cold stone of the prominent castle
looking down with vigour
and determination upon the flow of human cattle in the port.

The sea mist stripped the view of distant
yet so near Calais and was an analogue to the shrouds in my mind
making clarity of though an unavailable agony.

But I **loved** it all and so no need for change.

Anthony Lyng

Writers Peace

Sitting by the rippling brook
Tranquil minutes was all it took
Harboured words, lines unhired
A little piece of prose inspired.

Listening to the pigeons call
Watching insects so busy and small
Natures noise, man's content
All of this is heaven sent.

Looking across the fields of green
Nature's indelible pattern seen
Yellow rape and flowers wild
Pleasure for the Good Lords child.

Tranquil moments, man's desire
Set the human heart on fire
Harboured words, lines unhired
Grew to be a novel inspired.

Margaret Marshall

Sharing, or All This and Heaven Too

I counted my jumpers today. Does anyone ever need thirty?
You need one to take off and one to put on and one to change that
when it's dirty.
So I took them and gave them away, - to poor refugees who have
nothing;
To the young and the old to keep out the cold.
Yes, I counted my jumpers to-day.

I counted my money today. I really had more than I thought.
I've got some in the bank and some in the Pru and some in the box
beneath the bed too.
So I took it and gave it away to family and friends and to Oxfam;
To children in need and the hungry to feed.
Yes, I counted my money today.

I counted my blessing today; of these I have more than my share.
The love of a husband and family and friends, a home and a garden.
The list knows no ends.
So I'm trying to share them around - give comfort and heart to the
lonely;
And laughter and joy to the sad.

I've been given so much and I'm told at the end
I'll hear a voice say 'Welcome my friend,
This is my heaven - all you can see.
Come in faithful servant and share it with me'.

Marjorie Kewish

63

You Are ...

You're a ray of sunshine, on a cloudy day
You're my bottle of medicine, you take my pain away
You're my Northern star glittering on a moonlit night
You're my soothing reassurance in a nightmare full of fright
You're a rainbow in amongst the clouds
You're my security amidst my world of doubts
You're my knight in shining armour coming to the rescue
You're all my wildest dreams come true
You're the apple of my eye, the best thing to ever happen to me
I love you madly, now, always and forever.

Vanessa Galloway

Mind-Reader ...

With a puissant
indiscernible hand,
he explores my memory,
and rummages
through the fractures
and blemishes of time,
riffling through my past,
scouring
for past moral infractions,
he scrutinizes
my intrinsic self,
and my subconscious self
yields to his hand ...

Like a burglar
covertly creeping
through the night,
so behaves the intruder
within my mind;
imperceptible tentacles
prod and probe,
discovering sensitive portholes
to hidden memories,
unleashing once-forgotten tears,
once-forgotten smiles,
long-forgotten childhood years ...

Gary Hayes

Untitled

You can't wash away your fears and doubts
Cos life's complicated that's what its about
its strange to think that life's this way
doing things carefully not quite sure what to say
ambition, enthusiasm is our only survival
could this be a 60's 70's revival
together in love, peace and unity
in every town, village and inner city
to believe in something, someone and have faith
not to be known, be known and play safe
cos if you won't who will
its not worth staying put and still
stand up listen, learn and teach
for all you goals that you must reach
Get satisfaction, happiness and joy
cos we're here once, once only boy!

Tracie Amis

Sometime

Time, being relative to occasion,
Exists within the mind.
The briefest moment held in the memory
Is the same moment seeming to be endless.

What, then, is Sometime in our estimation
Which speaks of future acts?
Intentions which are quietly put aside,
Yet meaningful indeed.

The moment which will not again occur,
The lost opportunity.
Profound regret of missing that one chance,
Now finding it too late.

For people move away, and sometimes die
While we delay,
Relying on the Sometime just ahead
Of daily pursuits.

Sometime we will tell them that we love them,
Sometime speak of things
Deep in our hearts that we would wish to share -
An action or a thought.

Sometime I would have told the world of this
Forgetting to tell you,
Now finding it too late for your awareness,
For Time has passed
And you, no longer here, will never know
Of all these things.

This Sometime must be now and not postponed
Towards the coming morrow
Or we may lose the chance to show our care
And live with sorrow.

.

E Reynolds

The Questioner

When I lie in bed, asleep,
Do moonbeams touch my hair?
When I'm in another world,
Is my guardian angel there?

Do shooting stars
Aim their wishes at me?
Or do they forget
And just leave me be?

Do rays of starlight
Make night into dawn?
When twilight ends
Are sunbeams born?

Could unicorns be found
In this strange, strange world?
If we looked hard enough
Could dwarves to be unfurled?

Do peoples dreams and wishes
Ever really come true?
Using four - leaf clovers -
Will that really do?

Does Cupid really shoot arrows
From oh so high above?
And do the people that he hits
Really fall in love?

We have to realise, that some of these things,
We will probably never see,
All these questions are left unanswered,
And probably always will be.

P Pollero

When We Were Young

When we were young, the world was sweet, what simple lives we
led,
Toasting bread and knees by and open fire, gaslight, outside loo,
feather bed.
One doll or teddy, much loved. Mother sewed our frocks.
Knitted vests and jerseys. We girls knitted the socks.
Warm bread from the baker's van, we liked to feed his horse.
Picnics in the hay field, bread and jam, of course.
Gathering bluebells on our own, the scent still lingers now.
Nothing much to worry us, except the odd brown cow.
Blackberries and crab-apples, all carried home with pride.
We'd sit on the back of the coal-cart, to cadge a crafty ride.
They tarred the roads in those days. The smell was pungent ... sweet.
It rose in bubbles in summer, and the stones would stick to your feet.
We'd look for empty ciggie-packs, to find the odd fag-card.
Then see who could flick them farthest, out in the old back yard.
Walking back and forth to school, no cars were there for us.
Shank's pony served us well, not even a school bus.
We had to mind our teachers, and not speak out of turn.
A hundred lines was the penalty, so we'd very quickly learn.
Stirring the Christmas pudding, and having a lick of the spoon.
Making paper-chains and cards. It couldn't come too soon.
It always seemed to snow then, or so it seems to me.
Ice-patterns on the windows ... no central heating, you see.
Hot water bottles and soft eiderdowns,
Cocoa and bedsocks and flannel nightgowns.
The shops sold dolly-mixtures, bullseyes and licquorice wood.
Two ounces a penny, they were. We'd sample them all, if we could.
Treats were few and far between. Not much money about.
We'd sweep and dust and run errands, and take the babies out.
Happy days, all gone now. We've grown old and grey.
I think the youngsters miss a lot, in this so-called modern day.

Elsie Rogers

71

Sorry. To a Point

Sorry the words
were too sharp to hold
swords that sliced
deep and wounding,

Spears of abuse
thrown in vengeance
easily found
the softest ground,

Sorry yet I know
you deserved
every,
single,
pointed,
word,

Eye for an eye
for the pain
that burned through
days of silence
after parting,

the 'had time to think'
return,
sparked the potent fuse
words spat the air
blasting the second retreat,

Now you're afraid
that all is lost when
nothing is for certain,

still we may turn,
return again
to meet in a mutual light.

Gill Moore

The Orient Express

A relic of railway mystery,
a strip of chocolate and cream
sliding down the Darent Valley,
Pullmans posing for a poster
on Eynsford viaduct -
a study in speed
for Boys' Own Paper.
This re-created Oriental charm
threads through Kent's misty green.

Don't speak of its destination
or its silhouetted passengers -
all part of an art deco legend
disappearing round the curve of track,
beyond the tunnel, behind
the model railway scenery.

John Arnold

Ascendio Ad Absurdam

The man who
Wants to be
A member
Of the upper class

Gets drunk
In front of them
Because he hates
Them so much.

And all
The while they
Smugly let him
Buy them drinks.

Jock Mills

Stars

Stars in a velvet sky
Pinpoints of light.
Empty worlds passing by
Travellers of night
Seen by the naked eye
Twinkling bright.

Yvonne Cornwall

Christmas Eve

Fitful spurts of rain dashed errant wind,
Howling down the storm washed streets and lanes,
Rattling loose windows and door knockers,
Luring to a solid gust of salt spray and gale
Householders, fire warmed and TV drowsed.

High collared, deep pocketed, back to wall young men,
Waiting forlornly for dates who won't arrive, 'neath clocks
Speck dialled, showing a time that no one really heeds
Except for the quick glanced rush of hurrying crowds.

Stay. Somewhere in the aftermath of panic stricken storm
Is heard a noise, faint at first but waxing strong.
A jingling of bells, thudding of silver hooves,
A soft voiced growl ever urging on.
Who, seen by the pale light of stars, a robust, red-cheeked man.

Giver of joy and cheer for us, forever in our hearts,
A Peter Pan of life and love, a legend ever young.
Retold each year in humble home, and Palace nursery.
This heartfelt peace, a babies' laugh, lives on eternally.

Marjorie Chapman

Forever Seventeen

It seemed I only turned around,
And suddenly I was all grown up.
For seventeen seems so long ago,
Now that the overcoat of more mature years is wrapped around me.
Now mother, wife, lover, friend am I,
But I am always the secret youth,
I never felt I changed.
Still longing for my mothers arms to hold me and make the world
seem right.
To follow youthful whims,
And feel free to explore my dreams.
It seems my insides never caught up with my outward look.
I secretly think of my first loves,
To feel that tingle when fumbling hand touches breast.
To be without reservation.
To do what I want rather than what I know is right.
Why now the mature companion?
Rather the young man's fancy.
Where went my slender hip's?
Same to my upturned breasts.
When did laughter crease me so? I didn't notice.
Sometimes I hear the street music,
It catches my spirit and I start to move.
But then I catch myself and control overrides emotion.
Where once I danced now I appreciate.
So now I sit with my child held close and stroke her warm brow.
I am Mother and she is all I have been.
But I am always the secret youth
Forever seventeen.

Tracy Varndell

Untitled

Cindy you've gone to heaven
In pain you are no more
I know if someone's up there
They'll watch you that's for sure

You wasn't just a dog to me
To me you were so clever
I cannot praise you high enough
You should have lived forever.

But on that Thursday afternoon
You looked so ill to me.
I made my mind up there and then
That Friday it would be.

A friend of yours came in that day
Who always bought you Kit Kat.
He could see that you were ill
On your head did pat.

I stayed with you right to the end
Because I loved you so.
But you were just worn out and tired
And was ready to go.

You will be remembered
By everyone you knew
Mrs Martin and the rest
And especially by Sue.

Sue took photographs of you
I hope they turn out nice
However much I have to pay
They'll still be worth the price.

J King

The Divided Self

Only knowing
This chemical calm
Layer of tranquillity,
That smiles foolishly,
Papered over in pretty clothes
so the cracks don't show.

Someone is absent,
There is only
A ghost who looks the same
But the eyes have gone out,
Somewhere searching
But not here.

A passer-by
Struck by her own reflection,
A stranger, a loser
Intent on another impression,
She is walking lightly
And goes by my name.

Kathy Toop

81

Impressions in Sand

They were there last night -
  our footprints
sometimes running alongside
  when we were holding hands
sometimes jumbled together
  when we were following each other
sometimes far apart
  when we had nothing to say
sometimes running into the sea
  where we had cooled our ardour

They are not there today -
  our footprints
sand washed smooth by time and water
Gone - forever
But look; Over there -
Fresh Footprints

Beth Fender

My England

So small she lies amid the seas,
But her strength I know,
For I have seen her fight for right,
Yes, fight the greatest foe.

Her heart be pure, so doth her soul,
For with my eyes I've seen,
Her doors have opened wide to all,
Who in need have been;

She gave then love and shelter,
Helped them again to rise,
Oh my England! though so small,
Much bigger be thy size -

Jonathan Field

83

Time

Time is like a whirlwind.
Spinning round and round.
Time is like an ocean,
Wider than a sound.
Time is full of greatness
Failures. Faults. And woe.
Time is always everywhere,
Time that we all know.
Time is of the future
Also of the past.
Time is of the present,
Time will be the last.

D Rochester

Darkness

Darkness, hug me close,
Tight into your breast,
So I may hear your heartbeat,
Rhythmic,
Gently soothing,

So close, your arms around me,
I'm being drawn to you,
Into you,
Fears are fading,
Mountains become rocks, become sand,

Within this trust,
How I talk to you,
Plead to you,
Long for you,
The winds of silence are your soft reply

Don't leave me now I'm free,

Darkness, my light, my warmth,
Eternal strength,
Clasp my hands in shadows,
And hang our shame,
For we are one,

Unseen.

Mark Eaton

Why Don't we Care?

Roaming the streets all alone
The cats and dogs have no home

People have pets then throw them out
They have no heart without a doubt

For an animal or pet is for life
Not just a present for a child or wife

People don't care any-more in this world
When a cat or dog are even held

So think of these animals
starving, dirty and wet
They are not just a present
Their a lifelong companion and pet.

Anna Georgiou

86

A Question of Christmas

She tottered to the kitchen, feet on fire and hair awry,
Trying not to question once again the reason why.
She arched her back and stretched her arms and touched her aching
brow
Knowing that the next task was to stuff the bird somehow.
Thus complete and roundly stuffed with butter on its chest
She placed the poor plump creature alongside all the rest.
Where the mince pies and the Christmas cake, the trifle and the pud
The brandy butter, chocolate log and golden ham all stood.
The fridge was full to bursting, the table proudly set,
The silver gleamed, the woodwork shone, she felt so tired and yet ...
The house was full of luscious smells that seemed happy to combine,
Rich food mixed with lavender and candlewax with pine.
She felt a lifting of her heart and found that she could smile,
The glorious smell of Christmas made it suddenly worthwhile.
She wandered to the crowded lounge as she felt the feeling grow
And looking in she saw the tree, resplendent and aglow.
Beside it stood the ancient crib, her own from childhood days
And glancing up she saw the star of Bethlehem ablaze.
It shone down on them all from the top point of the tree
With the answer to the question she had been too tired to see!
Smiling round, she saw relief and love light up each face
The eager young, the older ones, lives led at quieter pace.
All gathered there to celebrate in the age-old family way
The birth of that most Special Child on that first Christmas Day.

Elizabeth Hardy

Divorce

When we were together and life wasn't grave.
it Seemed our Souls had something to Say,
to Say to each other all of the time,
I will be yours and you will be mine.
It Started through money What Can I Say?
it will haunt us till we all fade away.
then we remember just in time,
I will be yours and you will be mine.
then it got worse for better and worse,
you got the last word I got the first
it started us thinking was it all true,
Are you for me? am I for you?
then it's the end we both have to face,
Can we go on? Or give it away,
It's then we realise, all at one time,
I'm never yours and you're never mine.

S Ford

On Seeing a New Baby

Sweet cherished babe-so young, so pure, so new,
Endowed with love-the sun will shine on you!
Your every want your loved ones will provide,
What you need will gladly be supplied.
Unlike in other lands!

Not for you the perils of the gun-
Afraid to venture out into the sun,
Where neighbours fight across the garden wall,
And food is scarce, or there is none at all!
Such pleading hands!

The changing seasons pass as time goes by,
And marvel we, but still we wonder why
God in His Heaven lets the children hurt,
And fall, and bleed, upon their native dirt?
To what avail?

They have no voice to put the world to rights,
Their little eyes bewildered at the sights,
Their minds are troubled-cannot understand-
Why this destruction blights their lovely land!
And mourners wail!

Would we could stop, and wave a magic spell
To rid the world of hate, and anger quell.
So every babe can hope to live in peace,
And every black atrocity could cease!
But can it ever?

Barbara Hussey

Past Present and Future

So full of hope and longing,   *Past*
Why couldn't those times last?
Filled with laughter and smiles,
Why can't we live in the past?

I wish that I could see a future   *Present*
I wish I could not feel pain.
If all of my wishes could come true,
I wish I'd disappear like tears in the rain.

I am so scared of what's to come,   *Future*
So scared of the not knowing.
Most of all I'm scared because,
I don't know where I'm going!

Karen Rollins

90

Exiled by High Heels

I am an outcast from the human race,
no place for me at their table
piled with flesh and fish. Plied with blood and milk
they laugh at my lentils.

Conforming clowns stare at my plain clothes.
My unbent toes are rude, my bare face an affront.
If I will not wear fancy dress
they scorn my company.

My sacred life is isolate, church buildings
and mosques are unsafe havens.
My soul sings singly in the mass
Lest they vitiate my vision.

Commune with us, they beckon. Eat a dead cow!
Make yourself pretty, they coax. Cripple your feet in pointed shoes,
they urge, and worship orthodoxy.

Rasjidah St John

If Only

When I was small
I wished and wished
That someday I would be
A princess in a wonderland
For all the people to see
Where everyone was happy
With everything they dreamed
Would all come true for each of them
How silly children can be.
Now my younger days are fading
And my dreams are running out
There is no magic wonderland
There is no smiles about
But don't despair, no don't be glum
Deep down inside of me
I know that there's a Princess
Waiting to be free
To open up her castle for everyone to see
I may not do it in this world
But I'll do it in the next year you'll see.

Y Bell

No Reason Given

Ask not for explanations
When you read my book of verse
I do not wish to cause offence
My answer may be terse
I cannot always understand
The way I feel myself
I cannot stand discussions
Or want false compliment
Don't ask me what my reasons were
Or what I really meant
Don't let us have an inquest
Or post-mortem on the thing
My mind is no laboratory
No carcase to dissect
I have no armour plating
My feelings to protect.
I write just how I chanced to feel
At the moment of the thought
My thoughts are merely fleeting things
Not to be sold or bought
I try to express the pictures
That flicker through my brain
Like the dreams when one is sleeping
Why they come, one can't explain.

Naomi-Ruth Burden

God's Wonderful World

O there's noise in the world and darkness,
Sadness and tragedy,
Man's inhumanity to man
Is plain for all to see.

But as we sit down in the valley,
Gaze at the mountains tall,
We see the sheep with their lambs
And hear the cuckoo call.

The gentle breeze is stirring
The trees in summer dress.
O there's such peace in the valley
And calm and quietness.

White billowy clouds are rolling
Across a bright blue sky,
And the green grass of the hillside
Tells us of God on high.

Right up there on the mountain top
The air is fresh and free.
So is the love of our Father
Given to you and me.

His love is as high as a mountain,
His love is as wide as the sea,
And His arms are ever open
Enfolding you and me.

Eunice C Squire

Anxious Days

A scream of anger, a scream of fear
The naked faces that come so near
Haunting memories shadow behind
Giving up you'll fail to find
the serenity of a peaceful place
Where time goes by without a trace
The nudity of the eternal sky
Out of body we're free to die
Hidden reasons for countless doubts
Who know what this world's about

Juliette Seagrave

Regrets on a Winter's Day

Tonight the sea moves loud and thunderous,
And on my lips I taste the bitter spray
Thrown high into the air that cannot be still.
She, the future mother, bears her offspring in the womb
Like the closed bud borne on the thorns of roses.
In the darkness she is somewhere beside me.
I cannot see her, but I sense her telling me the child,
The pebble in the fish that has floundered by the tears of moonlight,
That on any other night would shine like candles,
But is this night robed in blackness and the sound of surf.
She is my lover who cannot be seen,
My space of dreaming that I bear upon myself
Heavy like the sleep in your eyes at dawn when birds sing,
When in the half-light of many rooms witness to your waking
The curtains shudder with departing thoughts.

The closed bud borne on the thorns of roses
Is wet with the dew of damp grass transparent as diamonds.
You have risen from the bed of dreaming
And stand by the window gazing out eastward to the sun,
Red as the blood that you hold for the child growing behind your
eyes.

I am at your side to hold you, soft as skin,
Cold as ice that in sleep had burned me.
The moonlight that tonight had deemed to shine
Has long since sunk under fields heavy in birth.
I could paint a hundred variations of this scene;
You, naked by your look-out,
With snow outside on the ground, the sky grey with its burden,
Daggers of ice pointing out the silence to you.
Or the sun, dim and low behind the distant trees
And leaves falling through the hands of wind that are sightless.
You are not changing for this moment of years.
For that there are many mornings yet to come like this.
E Jones

After the Telling

Sometimes when the black mood takes me
And my hands begin to shake
And I think of all you told me...
Then I know that I must break
Into a thousand screaming pieces
Each one lost and full of fear,
Something starts to cry inside me
And I long for you to care
With hugs and kisses
Passionate takings
Of my body when it seems
Nothing's left but broken promises
A broken heart and broken dreams.

J A Lock

Age

It's not elegant, you say, at my age,
to run. I should walk, glide, stand erect,
see that my hair is set and my clothes fashionable.
At my age I should 'have arrived'. I should not
act like a colt unbroken, or a girl untutored.
I should cease to be impulsive; should show restraint
and be well-garbed against uncertain weather.

But these are your ways - not mine.
I see too near me the impending gloom
of walking, gliding, standing.
I want the feel of wind within my hair:
to disregard my clothes and vault a stile.
I want to scuff my feet through rusted leaves,
And pit my strength against an angry sea.

I crave winged feet, as I once had.
I yearn to hear again the heartbeat
of the seasons' rhythm;
to feel the cold of winter on my face
and not to flinch.
Too soon I shall lie quietened, shall
rest with full restraint within another place.

M Jeffery

Spinster Looks Back

In memory's sharp cameo
A summer evening long ago;
A twisted branch against the blue,
And looking up at it with you,
And flooding into memory
All of young love's black misery,
The straining hope that knew at heart
That hope was hopeless from the start
And now a lifetime had gone by,
And we'd be strangers, you and I,
And now it couldn't matter less
And I look back with thankfulness.
My life has led in pleasant ways
Of friendship and of useful days
Only at times some incident
A casual word or tune or scent
Brings back the lost unhappy scene;
Nostalgia for what might have been

Helen Grundy

Rememberings

I look for you my love with eyes of memory
to fill my heart with pleasure as I see
You as you always were
Remembering too the way you looked for me.

Glimpses from the past impinge upon my mind
when a fleeting flash of love unsought
Turns back the clock, makes me catch my breath
As visions of you instantly are caught
To whirl inside my mind until I realise
Your sweet familiar self's no longer here
But only in my thoughts behind my eyes.

Then comes a sudden surge of grief
That takes me unaware
And plunges me to moments wet with tears
Just when I thought my inner self was calm
Able to admit the coming lonely years.
But as my memory stirs I see your face
And hear you voice again
And I am drowning in my private sea of pain.

It's said the heart will heal
And other avenues of life be opened up
But as I seek that future now I cannot see
Without your presence they will come to me.

But could it be possible, my dearest love,
that from these overwhelming bouts of grief
In time there will be moments of relief
And heartache slowly melt away
To leave but gentle love and sweet rememberings
To help me fill the empty corners of the day?

Sybil Steel

Thoughts of England

I travelled to Egypt - that far off land,
Saw the pyramids, sphinx and camels in the sand,
Gazed in awe at Pharaohs tombs in the Valley of the Kings
And marvelled at the painting of many wondrous things.
I saw the great Colossus seated on his throne,
The palaces of Karnack - the greatest ever known,
Great temples built at Philae looking down the Nile,
But still I thought of England - just for a little while.

Then I journeyed on to Greece, home of ancient myths.
I saw the lovely Parthenon and the great Acropolis,
The Oracle of Delphi - the navel of the Earth.
Then on to the stadium where Olympic games gave birth,
Temples built to Zeus and Hera, Mycenaes golden mask,
The market square at Corinth where St Paul resumed his task.
I saw the blue Aegean and its legend made me smile,
But still I thought of England - just for a little while.

I returned to England with its cold, grey sky and sea
And saw the Roman Castles built to keep the island free.
The beautiful cathedrals and the Saxon mounds,
King Arthur's rugged Cornwall beyond the Plymouth Sound.
I saw the Tower of London and the Palace of the Queen,
The march past of the Royal Guard - the smartest ever seen!
The silver flowing rivers and the Kentish woods for miles
And I thought I'd stay in England for more than just a while!

V Garratt

101

I Don't Want to Get Involved

They had a fight last night
You could hear it through the walls
She was crying
He was shouting
And throwing plates around the room

But I don't want to get involved
I keep myself to myself
It's better that way
It's none of my business anyway - is it?

They had a fight again last night
I could hear it through the walls
The voices were higher
The noises were louder
And not just plates this time - but chairs

They had yet another fight last night
I could hear it all through the wall
She was screaming
Then a loud bang
Like a sack of potatoes flung against the door
Then nothing more...

The ambulance came late last night
Siren wailing down the street
They wheeled her out on a stretcher
A blanket over her face
'I'm sorry officer - I never heard a thing!'

David Chapman

Seaside Dream

I must go down to the sea again
To the beautiful Island of Thanet
Where if you have a good idea
The council promptly ban it.

Where condoms rush in on the evening tide
And the beach is covered in plastic
Where the sight of the sewage floating by
Is really quite fantastic.

I must go down to Thanet again
And attend a council meeting
where every decision that has to be made
Is eased by a Masons greeting.

Where most of the shops in the High Street are closed
Because they've doubled the rents
And where Edwardian Hotels once stood
The plots are hired out for tents.

I must go down to the sea again
For soon there'll be nothing left
And the white tipped waves that moved my soul
Appear to be covered in Dreft.

The golden beaches are emptier now
For it's cheaper to go to Spain
the leisure industry's gone to the wall
Our loss is Benidorms gain.

Jane Mirams

Walton on Thames Local Shop Keepers

These few names, I conjure from the past,
not knowing, that they would not last,
Dick Birkhead, selling bike and bell,
ladies undies, sold by Mr Smith and Mr Snell,
Bread from Lee's, Cousins and Mr Brown
Waldens, Smallridges, best fish in town
selling clothes, Mr Huntley and Mr Marshall's
and Mr Bell, for childrens uniforms for schools
Kidman Mann and Mr Purdie, selling houses were their things,
While Mr Mayer, sold watches and rings
Miss Annett, Mr Sexton, selling china and glass,
Whilst Solleys fish and chips, you could not surpass.
Mr Grimditch, Mr Ridge sold meat
and Mr Frisby, put shoes on you feet
John Windsor, and A E Clarke, for ironmongery and tools
Hills for tobacco, and booking seats for music halls
While Mr Turner, for cars and their needs
Hutchinson, House and Aegers, for corn and seeds
or to the bookies for K H Price.
Paynes and Boynes for sweets and ice,
and for a treat, we had three
Regent, Regal, and Odeon for you and me.
Then again, plenty to choose
Like, Castle, Crown, Apps Court Tavern, in which to booze
in Walton, where I was born and grew
most of these people, it was I knew.

Peter Brewer

The Old Harbour
(Pagham)

The harbour still before my eyes
Bereft of sea the salt marsh lies;
Wheatears strut on the old stone wall
Little terns tooing and froing, call.

An empty expanse of mud and sky
And overhead the wild geese fly.
Like liquid silver the sea returns
Claiming her own, as one who yearns.

A rosey glow tints the west,
Tipping with gold the white waves crest
And suddenly the air is full of sound
As birds to their roosting abound.

Then through the misty gloom I see
Tall ships making for the quay;
Ghostly sails slack, running with the tide
Phantoms now as silently they glide.

The old harbour in a shroud sleeps
A lone heron his watchful eye keeps.
The mirage fades as darkness falls,
Across the moonlit water a curlew calls.

Patricia Emery

The Boy in the Wheelchair

To me it is a pleasing sight
To watch somebody fly a kite,
And see it dancing in the sky,
However does it get so high?

I saw one flying yesterday,
As through the park I made my way,
I stopped and watched a little lad
Flying it, helped by his dad.

When just about to walk away
I saw another watcher there,
He used his hands to shade his eyes
As he looked up into the sky -
A helpless lad in a wheelchair.

The boy and dad had seen him too,
And then they did a kindly thing.
The kite still flying in the sky,
I felt a tear well in my eye,
They asked that lad to hold the string.

What joy! I saw on the lad's face;
And from his lips came joyful sound.
He held on the string so tight,
His eyes were dancing with delight
Until the kite at last came down,
They gave the happy boy their kite,
And left him laughing with delight.

Bob Squire

Numb Reality

One sad and mixed up lady
Once lived in that house too
Her children - four so beautiful
Could now belong to me or you.

Taken into care you see
That sad lady passed away
Left with nothing but her drink
Died one sad and painful day.

The children put up for adoption
Like puppies up for sale
I won't tell you anymore yet
'Cos it's a long and painful tale.

C Ottley

Rocks at Futami

Not so long ago
off the coast of Japan
(I think it was Japan
I think it was),
two lonely rocks
stood close together
but apart.

And the fishermen
of the tiny coastal town,
clad in loincloths
and bands around their hair,
saw those rocks
yearning towards each other
in the sea.

They set out in their boats
those salty men,
with heavy coils of rope,
(I think they took some wine
I think they did),
and looped the rope
first round the small
and then around the larger rock,
and married them forever
in the sea.

Beth Porter

108

Reflections

Reflections in a mirror as I pass by
Throw back the face and form I wish to see
I look deep within the glass and concave shell
Do I see you standing there beside me?

The grey swirling mist creates your presence
Or are these just my wishes coming to the fore
I've looked for you in dreams and distant shadows
When my eyes were full and my heart was sore

Your shadows always on the outside of my senses
I feel it always and it will always grow
I touch the glass, my sigh mists your reflection
I look down, and at my feet a perfect velvet rose.

Unicorn

Answers to the Questions (You Were Afraid to Ask)

there's a voice in the mirror inviting you to step inside
and meet your alter ego waiting on the other side
with the answers to the questions
you were afraid to ask
all put in perspective
through the bottom of a glass
So the Shadowman's
holding out his hand
to lead you to a Shadowland
of graffiti scarred
and mirrored bars
of faces framed in silhouette
where the old drink to remember
and the young drink to forget
there's hope for tomorrow but tomorrow never comes
cause hell has frozen over so you stay with the one
with the answers to the questions
you were afraid to ask
all put in perspective
through the bottom of a glass

Clive Gardner

Seasons of the Sea

Dusted ice on frozen pebbles.
Till the sea rolls in to wash the shore.

Lukewarm sun on lonely footprints,
till the sea rolls in to wash the shore.

Summer's might tans ashen bodies,
till the sea rolls in to wash the shore.

A golden shadow on fading daylight,
till the sea rolls in to wash the shore.

Forgotten sandle, plastic carton tangled line on broken tree,
the shore this time must wash the sea.

David J Strawbridge

Dream

To explain a dream is easy, but also very hard.
A never ending story, or a very long path.
For yourself only to know, things you can't explain or show.
Daring, passion, excitement and lots of fun.
Scary, sad, things that make you run.
But sometimes you can forget what you even did or said.
Your dream is always over once you have awoke.
You never have that same dream, the story line is broke.

Nadine Strawbridge

It's you

The hasty kiss and the flying feet,
A farewell wave as I run to meet,
An awaiting train that will take me to,
A place that is lonely for there is no you.

The return to the barracks how lonely the ride,
Time passes slowly for you're not by my side,
Yet the scenes that I love are there for my view
I turn round to whisper and find there's no you.

A twist of a dial and here we are talking
The day is so lovely we should be out walking
Treading the green grass still wet with the dew
But here we are talking and still its not you.

The heartache the sorrow these things that I see
Form part of lifes highway the human comedy.
Time drags so slowly, but soon you'll be due
I hear a voice whisper, I turn, and it's you.

I Hardy

Passing Time

An aching heart, no love, all pain
Dependency the enemy,
Longing one day to be free
I'll never wish for youth again.

Life moves on and love's refrain
Builds hopes and hearts desire,
When peace within can quell the fire
I still won't wish for youth again.

All dreams it seems one can attain
Fulfilment found at last,
With life's dilemmas' in the past
I'll never wish for youth again.

And so life's course begins to wane
Contentment charms the soul,
Though passing years may take their toll
I still won't wish for youth again.

Oh aching limbs, no hope, disdain
A feeble body, troubled mind,
Hoping someone will be kind
I truly wish for youth again.

Patricia Firmin

Amberley (South Downs)

We will walk but once these well walked hills,
These trodden paths where tread the ancient feet.
Be familiar once with the secrets held
In this unfamiliar sacred ground.
For ancestral memories linger here, abound
Where rivers weave through a patchworked land
Across this our tribal home.
We can pray but briefly at these altars,
Once for worship, risen up before us now,
Cathedrals where we stand.
Monuments raised to nameless gods forgot,
Temples splendid then, still splendid yet,
When viewed with endless, ageless sight,
When watched through older eyes.

Evelyn Holden

The Storm on Shakespeare Beach

Summer is here! Do you think that is true?
Or are we mistaking those clouds in our view?
Do you remember the days that have flown,
When hot days seemed endless and rain was unknown?

Or do we think only of good times to tell,
Forgetting that bad days did happen as well?
We seem to remember that holiday fun
Was always accompanied by blue skies and sun.

Was it so?

I seem to remember one day one the beach
We children were climbing 'mong rocks within reach,
When suddenly rain came and spoiled our play,
And shelter was sadly some distance away.

As we turned back to run, the lightning was flashing,
The waves became rough and the thunder was crashing;
Our earlier play with the sandcastles spoiled,
Our packed lunches soaked and our clothes wet and soiled.

It did not last long - half an hour at the most,
At Shakespeare the clouds soon pass over the coast.
But we had to get home, and get things put to rights.
To climb up the steps, and then round to the heights.

The sun now, so hot, we dried out as we went,
We remember how that day of summer was spent...

... But now they must find somewhere else for their fun:
The beach is redundant - *The 'Chunnel' has come!*

D M Cook

Your Warmth

You lie
softly breathing
face
breath
warm.
You are silent
and yet I see thoughts racing
through, round across
but not out of
your mind.
Your eyes are closed
your body still.
Beauty pours out
making me feel
comfort in your warmth.

Your face
is warmth.
Your body
is warmth.
Your word
is warmth.
And yet,
your mind
will not accept me.
Trust me
As I do you.
Let me in
And I will too.

Trudi Dunlop

... And Tears Fell

She searched
desperately grasping
at any familiar memory.

She wanted to search
and to find
and to find.

And she found a sense
of isolation,
yet belonging,
to a society in which she was adamantly
involved
and comforted
yet lost.

Cut off from a world who infinitely cared.
Caring reduced to an inevitable occurrence,
a natural progression.

And outside it rained
Heavy, long drops of water
pounding the earth.

Sleep overwhelmed her mind
and a vampire
swooped his black cape around his body
to leave but a bat
free to fly until it was time to return.

Samantha Dunlop

Rubbish

Rubbish rubbish rubbish, old cars and rusted tins
Man alone makes rubbish like these and other things.

Rubbish rubbish rubbish, aerosols with Cfc's
Man alone makes toxins that kill the forests' trees.

Rubbish rubbish rubbish, plastic that will not rot
Man alone for the environment, it seem cares not a jot.

Rubbish rubbish rubbish, rubbish piling high
Man alone makes rubbish that will make our planet die.

Valerie Nadin

Dream Dance

Each bend of painful joints needs special care,
Measure the weight the knee will have to bear;
Stair treads have to be thought and rehearsed,
Where two at a time was once a careless youthful burst.
The nearest shop seems twice as far now to go,
But I start with jaunty walk saying 'not too slow';
Weighing the shopping bag from an aching arm,
Lifting it cautiously to limit any harm.
I rattle the pill bottle, rub in the cream;
Twist round my stick, and dance like a dream.

Hot iron torture thrusts right in the spot,
Skewers the shoulder when weeding the plot.
Half rolled in bed brings the painful gasps,
As stiffening joints feel like scraping rasps.
Think about early rising but creak like a wreck,
Even careful dressing jars every bone in the neck.
So easy to spend all the time dwelling on pain;
Keep moving somehow helps beat the energy drain.
I rattle the pill bottle, spin in a trance;
Trip over the stick, and dream of the dance.

Tom Chorlton

A Sad Tale - But True

I stopped the car beside that tree,
Of almost perfect symmetry,
Heard bees amidst the yellow broom,
Yet I was filled with fear and gloom,
Because I'd heard that day, you see,
The dreaded word, redundancy.

To calm my fretful, worried brain,
I looked towards that tree again,
No lord of park where river flowed,
This layby on a country road,
Was furnished with a rubbish bin,
With lid on top to keep it in.

Swift movement from the tree - a blur,
Of bushy tail and red-brown fur,
Which reached the bin and gently slid,
Climbed up to just beneath the lid,
Intent on food from which to sup,
The squirrel heaved the cover up.

A sandwich, large, the creature found,
And with it sprang down to the ground.
Triumphantly he took a bite,
Then from the tree, in hurried flight,
Three crows appeared, flew low to steal
The squirrel's hard-to-come-by meal.

Fur bristling with frustrated fright,
He lost that fierce, uneven fight,
My sorrow for his hungry pain,
And sorry for myself again,
Yet I will never hungry be,
While there's Social Security.
M Le Petit

Little Love

For you I feel affection, like a little bud
I hope that this affection will blossom into love
And when our love's in flower, may the petals never fall
but be forever springtime and not hear winters call.

Natalie Andrews

On the Somme

The noise of the battle is over
And silence descends on the land,
There's peace on the face of that soldier
We see lying there on the sand.

No sound from those pale lips are uttered,
Or flicker from eyelids half-closed,
Blonde hair blowing soft in the chill wind
As if for a painting, he'd posed.

Where did you come from young soldier?
Who waited for you to come home
From the war to end wars? as they promised
Back to land from which you'd ne'er roam.

Perhaps there's a letter you cherished
In the pocket right next to your heart,
And a photo you gazed at with longing
So often since you were apart.

It was on the TV that we saw you
With an old man, who cried bitter tears
As he spoke of the comrades he'd lost there,
And the mud, and the pain, and the fears.

It's many long years since you fell there
But the world's never stopped talking 'bomb',
We haven't learnt much in between, lad,
Poor handsome young man on the Somme.

Esther Barry

The Smoker

Why don't you give it up my friend
That dirty smoking habit.
You were eager when you started
And didn't think that it
Would finally be a deterrent
To the life that you enjoy.
How foolish and unenlightened you were
When you were a boy.
You couldn't wait to have a puff
Spent hours in the loo
Puffing away and feeling sick
And now that day you rue.
Foolhardy, in spite of feeling sick
Now the habit you cannot kick.
Ignoring all the warnings
You know you're being foolish
Because one day will come the time
When smoking will you finish.
Why don't you heed the warnings
You know it all makes sense
And if at last you give it up
You will be recompensed.

Evelyn Evans

The White Horse (Uffington)

On the side of a hill, on the
rolling downs is a horse, a white
horse which is like no other horse
anywhere else to be found. In size
so large that with but a few steps
it would cover the hill on which it
is to be found. A horse which neither
you or I could ever ride although we
could both sit on its back, but not
astride. Lay on its head and even take
rest under his hocks, but alas not a horse
you or I could ever ride. A horse which
never takes a stride, never canters, trots
or walks. A horse which remains permanently
inclined on its side. A great white horse
cut out of chalk on a grassy slope.
Not a horse to ride.

Peter Young

Untitled

I've climbed right to the top now,
The pinnacle of fame
And the powers that be have given me
A 'handle' to my name.

I've struggled hard for years and years
And cared not for a soul
And no one dared get in my way
Until I reached my goal.

But sometimes in the dead of night
I say a little prayer
For those whose backs I've trampled on
While I was getting there.

K Blake

126

The Baby-sitter

She was a lovely little girl,
as white as was the snow,
the smile it was so innocent,
then her parents had to go.
A wicked glint formed in her eye,
the smile turned to a frown,
she rampaged screaming round the room,
she just would not calm down.
She jumped on all the furniture,
pulled her poor dog's ears,
the baby-sitter shouted,
and then burst into tears.
The girl was such a naughty child,
and ignoring the sitter's pleas,
proceeded to write on the wallpaper,
and paint faces on her knees.
The baby-sitter started screaming,
'I can't take anymore'
the girl heard a noise and sat down,
smiling sweetly as mum walked in the door.
'Oh mum it's been so horrible,
she shouted at me and I cried,
why did you go and leave me?'
She sobbed, as tears rolled down from her eyes.
So let this be a warning,
if you're baby-sitting tonight
the innocent child before you,
may not be all sweetness and light...

Hazel Edginton

An Easter Message

I gaze in wonder at the things I see each spring;
The air is fresh and all is clean and gay;
The grass a brilliant green appears as carpeting,
While here and there a crocus or a twig does lay.

Once walking o'er the rich green grass I found,
Just one such twig cast from a broke bough;
From top to earth it fell and rested on a mound;
It lay there purpose gone, to slowly die now.

I picked it up and held it, turning it about;
A piece of wood, once living but now dead;
And as I looked I saw a bud was coming out,
The wood lived yet and on the spring it fed.

I kept this wondrous twig and strolled across the lea
To where a tiny Church gave haven, peace and rest;
I passed beneath the lych and through the Western door
To see the Eastern Chancel window lit the West.

I moved along the Nave and stood beneath the Rood
The Blessed Cross - dead wood but holding life,
That too was wood, once living but now dead;
But in its lifeless arms, life hung to strive.

That bud however grew, for the Cross of wood though dead;
Did cradle life, the early Church to grow.
'If I be lifted up' His voice a promise said
'Will draw all men to Me' that love and life will flow.

Thus Easter gives a message to this earth in spring;
That winter's past and death has gone with strife;
We can all grow in peace and love will bring
Us safely through this vale to Greater Life.
Henry Pugh

The Burglar

Who guards a burglar's house when he goes out at night?
Does it bristle with alarms to give his mates a fright?

Who buys the stolen TV's he sells in clubs and bars,
or the multitude of radios he's nicked from people's cars?

Do they have a secret handshake, on house and car a sign,
which protects their goods and chattels but unfortunately not mine?

When the houses of the honest lie empty and bereft,
everything has been stolen and nothing has been left,
have nots have become haves and haves become have nots,
will we go round to their house to see what they have got?

Pauline Brennan

Untitled

I'm going to be a traffic cop
Put stickers everywhere
I'll get all those blighters
Who park where I don't dare

They sit on double yellow lines
There's not a cop in sight
I'd give them all a summons
And say it serves you right

I won't care if they're rude to me
Nor punch me on the chin
I'll take it like a hero
And then I'll run um in

I'd clear all roads in England
It wouldn't take me long
But they would all be back again
The minute I was gone

B W Pantling

The Library

My home is in the library
Where I sit upon the shelf
Between 'A World of Daisies'
And 'A Guide to Better Health'

I am an old edition
And my pages are quite torn
But my story is unequalled
And goes back to days of yorn

In between my well worn pages
Lifes' history unfolds
And the story that I tell
Means more than jewels and gold

The oaths of Kings and Princes
Have been made upon my cover
And men for generations
Have been proud to call me brother

But when man is in deep trouble
And find's life hard to bear
I am the comfort that he needs
In me there's one who cares

My stories scan the sands of time
Scripted in days of old
By aged, stooped and weary monks
Lifes' story to unfold

I sit here in the library
I know I have no rival
I am the base of all mankind
I am the *family bible*
Valerie Sparks

'Twas on a Monday Morning, Oh!

'Twas on a Monday morning, oh - that I beheld the chaos, oh,
That everyone'd created, oh, the weekend now gone by;
The books, the socks, the homework, oh, that could not be located,
oh,
Dashing away to school and work - dashing away to office, oh,
Dashing away to college, oh, to leave the house awry.

'Twas on a Tuesday morning, oh - that I beheld the washing, oh,
The shopping and the cooking, oh, with positive distaste.
The cleaning and the mending, oh, the weeding of the patio,
Dashing away with hoover, oh, dashing away with trowel, oh,
Dashing to pay the milkman, oh, 'tis hurry, rush and haste.

'Twas on a Wednesday morning, oh - that I beheld the traffic, oh,
A-grinding to a snarl-up, oh, before my very eyes.
Would I be late to get to school to meet the kids? (the general rule).
Dashing away to shoe shop, oh, dashing away to dentist, oh,
Dashing away to music, oh, I wonder, am I wise...

'Twas on a Thursday morning, oh, yours truly over-sleepeth, oh,
The household fell to pieces, oh, and tempers were affray.
A sandwich box forgotten, oh, and couldn't find the car key, oh;
Dashing away with the dog to vet, dashing away my hair to set,
Dashing away to - I forget! (Perhaps I'll go away).

'Twas on a Friday morning, oh - the car it failed to start, ho! ho!
The big end's on the blink, oh no, it really is a pain.
The children's medical at school; I told my aunt that I would call...
Dashing away to pay the bills, dashing away to library, oh,
Dashing away to school once more, 'tis wonder that I'm sane.

'Twas on a Saturday morning, oh - that daughter sprained her ankle,
                                                                    oh
And couldn't go to Brownies, oh, and sulked the morning through.
I served behind the counter, oh, at jumble sale for Oxfam, oh,
Dashing away with bags of goods, dashing away with loaded car,
Dashing away to get back home, to cook the dinner, too.

On Sunday, he said, 'and what have you been doing all week, then?'

Linda E Bending

133

In the Dog-House

Our Councillors are met in solemn session;
Our Council is engaged in grave debate.
The subject it's discussing with such passion
Is one on which depends our very fate.

What can it be? It isn't schools or houses;
It isn't taxes, refuse, roads or jobs.
It isn't crime or poverty that rouses
Such fierce reforming zeal, oh no -- it's *dogs!*

It seems that man's best friend is in the dog-house;
Man's dear old faithful pal is in disgrace.
You see, he doesn't always use the bog-house;
He sometimes goes in quite the naughtiest place.

But never fear, our Council will defend us.
Its vigilant protection never ceases.
The battle it'll fight will be tremendous
To save us from the frightful threat of faeces!

T V Newmark

S S Tranquillity

My ship is called Tranquillity.
She's set to sail upon a sea
Of calm with gentle dignity.
If you would care to come aboard,
The price is what you can afford.
If you can lend a helping hand
To trust one another to understand

To hoist the flag of liberty.
And navigate a world that's free.
Light the port and starboard lamps,
Sailing forth - no special ranks.
To find an ocean filled with love.
Then you are welcome; step aboard!

Pamela M Dean

Antipathy

She's like a witch, with her nose thin
and hooked; dressed in black, always black,
and a voice like a magpie on heat.
Eyes like a magpie as well; they flick green,
here and there, always flicking; in shops,
on the bus, in the street.
Nobody likes her.

He's just a scrot, an old wrinkled hung-under
limp, baggy reject from Exit;
his lips always slaver; they dribble
in rivers whenever you see him
outside... fair or storm, cold or warm.
He slavers wherever you see him, forever.
And nobody likes him, either.

The weirdest of couples, a kind of ensemble
of scruffy ill-favour. They whiff
of their lifestyle; pig-rearing and smoking;
chain smoking, not fags or like that
... just the ket they keep growing
up there on their holding.
No wonder that nobody likes them.

They grimace and scuttle away when they
see me; scuttle so fast I've a feeling
they're leery. Of me? That's a
good one. It's me should be running. Me?
Running? That's really a good one... crutch leg,
a patch-eye and my bagpipey wheezing?
How come they don't like me?

Lal Mineham

136

Progress

A ballad was written
In years gone by.
It told of people
And a heartfelt cry.

Now we have papers
And radio too
Of Mr Bloggs
Ah and who are you?

The village next door
Seemed far afield
And news of London
It really appealed.

Now we have satellite
Telephone of course
People all talking
Until they are hoarse.

But what do we know
Of the people next-door.
Oh turn off the telly
It's only a bore.

Rosemary J Povey

Landscapes

Green the cat's eyes sparkling brightly in the hedgerow late at night,
Green the sea-tide sighing softly with the chill of winter's bite,
Green the grass of village cricket, batting chaps there dressed in
white,
Green the glass of bottles clinking, thrown outside the pub at night,
Green my car with polish gleaming, windows clear and chromium
bright,
Green the wheatfield rippling lightly, up the lane there on the right,
Green this country, green all over, no desert here so we're all right.

Brown the skins of men who live here, in the glare of sunshine
bright,
Brown the earth and bare the landscape, nothing here but dust to bite,
Brown the babies, tums distended, flies infecting tears and sight,
Brown the uniforms defending, nothing here of shining white,
Brown the trucks for food supplying, till some gun sets them alight,
Brown the dusty tents for shelter, dying place for sick at night,
Brown this country, brown all over, how can we say we're all right?

Jean Mabey

The Bird Man

'High seas, narrow seas, home seas,
Baltic, Adriatic...',
Under the monument he pauses,
Stooped, arthritic.
Pigeons cluster at his feet,
Crumbs spray from gloved hands.
Shoppers sweep past, unseeing, uncaring.
Only the pigeons gather round,
Some maimed and grounded,
Emitting their monotone, dull, unvaried.
A salty gust sweeps up from the sea,
In a grey cloud the birds scatter.
The worn old medals clash softly
As he lifts his fingers
To trace the mossy inscription -
'High seas, narrow seas, home seas...

Judy Pavier Wilson

Castrato

At dawn was there crisp fragrance
as hope hung from each bending bough,
expectant youth and spring light
as backdrop to a stage of promise?

Harlequin has vanished forever
his glorious colours faded away
as Pierot's ghost shed tears of black
for friend and gallery long departed

Love's inspiring overture
became a distant fugue
for those en route to oblivion
locked in chests with masks and years

How real the danger when life spills
through vital holes needed to breathe?
Stagnant pools cannot spawn life
yet death soon breaches tidal waves

Free potent lives risk infection
is creative thought a lethal germ,
for carriers are spurned as outcasts
unfulfilled in voiceless poverty?

Conventional even is this verse
and fleeting the reflective moods
of understudies with terminal stage fright.
Must pure expression die intestate?

Jonathan Pyke

Infinite Peace

Let there be no lamentation
from loved ones when I die,
but rejoice in tears of gladness,
for I shall suffer pain no more
and relinquish all sorrows
and burdens of the past,
I shall exalt in celestial rest,
an immortality of infinite peace.

Brenda Axworthy

A Poem of Sadness

The leafy mountains reach up to the clouds of smoke belched by the
never ending chimneys of industry.
The poor terrace houses stretch out with no end-out onto the polluted
sea.
A curious mixture of Welsh mountains like beautiful green puffy
clouds, industrial work and a never-ending caterpillar of terraces.
A saddening sight
Such scenery yet spoiled by the greedy companies of power.

Carolyn Bland

142

Avoid

No more words to say.
It has all been said too often.
They have been repeated frequently.
Time and time again
All has been spoken,
Echoed, written printed -
Shouted, whispered,
Said from here to there
Accumulated endlessly.

Now write no more,
Nor say.
Just hark and listen.
How peaceful silence is.
There's so much else
Unheard before.
Let words and failure go.
There is something else -
Listen.

Jane Evans

Sleepless Night

Sleep why don't you close my eyes?
And take me to your fantasy world,
Where all things are possible.
Cover me with the gossamer shimmering sheet of sleep.
Where my father will hold me tight
Where reality is a dream,
Where men do not fight,
Where love is not lust.
Let my mind be calm,
And my body still,
So I may face another day.
Sleep enfold me.

Margaret Fitchett

Air

You may heat it or freeze it or try to blow it away
you can breathe it or compress it for later when at play
then you can pump it into your bed or into your tyre
or use it with matches and wood to warm by the fire

You can use it to float on in colourful hot air balloons
you can float down to earth on it with the other buffoons
then use it to give lift when as through it you fly
you can expel it with gusto when you've had too much pie

Without it the woodwind would be very sadly deplete
and the birds and the bees would then suffer defeat
bringing life as we know it to a halt and despair
and all because someone had stolen the air

You can make it smell fresher with use of a spray
or clean it with filters that will clog up one day
then you can mix it with N^2O to give you a laugh
or force it through water when you're taking a bath

If you heat it it rises if you cool it it falls
compress it it shrinks but you then need thick walls
because the pressure increases too much to then bear
it is what life's all about good clean fresh air.

R N Carpani

Nature at its Best

Sitting in my window looking out,
I can see what nature is all about.
The beauty of the flowers and trees,
To the beholder can only please.
Shrubs and bushes of various greens,
Flowers in borders give multicoloured scenes.
Bees humming around their chosen plant,
Give rise to a pleasant gentle chant.
Conifers stand erect and tall,
Majestic, rising overall.
The rockery made up from coloured stone,
Where heathers and miniature plants are grown.
To make it more attractive too,
Gnomes are placed for all to view.
Bird boxes hang from makeshift trees,
Filled with water and assorted seeds.
What a joy to watch the birds fly in,
Pecking away and chirruping.
Then down amongst the flower-beds, worms they've found,
From recently turned over ground.
Overhead, branches sway gently in the breeze,
From the many overhanging trees.
Out of its hutch, a rabbit crosses the grass,
Scurries away when anyone comes past.
Enjoying its time of being free,
Hopping in and out under the tree.
Overhead the sky so blue,
Looks down upon this peaceful view.
Nature in all its glory shown,
In the garden of my home.

Jeannette Rose

Walking Through Moments

Into a summer's evening we walked
attuned to every murmur we talked
our way through dinner dances of midges
while the hedges simmered with fruit
our hands and lips disintegrated in juice.

Over the un-estated fields we climbed
to voice our thoughts in the sky's expanse of time
the cows licked our legs as we shadowed
the sound and light of evening down
under the snoring rookery and into town.

Today the cars on the ringway cruise or crawl
as across the estates the sunshine strolls
I watch the headstones in the cemetery
sketch our mortality in the shade
and all my finger-stained elation fades.

Sarah Hamblett

147

Much a Do

Dogs will be dogs and must do what they do,
But why does it have to end up on my shoe.
I can't always look where I'm putting my heels,
And when pushing a pram it sticks to the wheels.

In Spring and Summer I favour the sandal,
But fresh 'do' 'tween toes I cannot handle.
Excreta abounds on footpath and verge,
And some of the parks are ripe for a purge.

Could scoops be imposed, or is that beyond hope.
Call me 'old sober-sides' but its not a joke.
The blind clean up what their dogs have to do,
I'll follow their footsteps 'till you do to.

Jean Hands

Wisdom

Wisdom does not mean knowledge
To say so puts wisdom to shame
It's the fool who belittles wisdom
By carelessly calling it 'Brains'

Knowledge is gained through learning of facts
Wisdom obtained with time
For knowledge is accumulation of memory
And wisdom, acquisition of mind

Selay Hassan

Yorkshire Contacts

There is nothing like that Yorkshire desolation,
the starkness of the moorland in a wind...
the pitiful frustration of a spirit -
the proud, repressive shyness of their kind...
the sudden cold withdrawal of a nature
worn threadbare by persisting years of toil;
the seeming sterility of Yorkshire:
the grudging fertility of its soil!

There is nothing like the friendliness of Yorkshire -
the pervading flood of kindness from the soul...
There is nothing like the blaze of Yorkshire laughter -
the sudden spurt of flame from Yorkshire coal...
Its abundance when its spirit has received you -
the bounty of its working-people's hearth;
The wordless directness of their welcome
when you have learned to raise a Yorkshire laugh!

M E D Grason

The Forest of the Mind

The hazy sunshine filters like
a familiar mist through the
twisted and gnarled branches.
As two lovers their trunks entwine
forming an inseparable bond of
unbearable passion.

In his mind he sees the clearing
where he stood, recapturing that moment
as his brush caresses the canvas.
Immobile he stands, his thoughts unfolding
into the chosen
medium of art
from whence he knows not what will happen.

He steps back, no photograph, no sketch
all that he has is in his mind.
Stored within is an elaborate picture
observing everything in its minutest detail.

The picture is talking,
telling all who pass
a very different story...its own story.

Ad infinitum...
Each stroke obsessive in its strength,
the subtle hints of brown, green and yellow
decisive in their obscurity.

Alex de Mierre

Windows of the Soul

When you look into someone's eyes
And you see beyond the colour
You enter a very private place
The person you discover
There before you are secret fears
Precious thoughts, internal tears
Locked away, tight, secure
Only a special person
May unlock the door
Many don't realize a door is there
Others do but just don't care
Or do not look - only stare
These people are blind and unaware

Julie MacDonald

Christmas Eve Again

The only light was the silver star
And the world waited.
In here the future was secure
Safe in the existence of The Two -
The son, The daughter.
Success anticipated.

The parcels, bulky and intriguing,
Circled the tree,
Dragged from its nourishing cold
Into their safe heat.
Thoughtlessly dying.
Withering, thorny.

SHE might be a dancer - pink ballet shoes
For special toes,
A rag doll to nurse and comfort
To imitate a mother's love
In perpetuity.
All tied with bows.

And everywhere the repeated ritual.
Preparation done
Fondly tired, sure and satisfied,
All givers slept, awaiting the morning,
Cherishing expected responses.
But they gave the boy a gun.

Pamela Courtney

Starry Night
(Vincent Van Gogh)

Meteorite crescendos, luminous comets,
starry catherine wheels,
circumscribe their confined canvas.
Whirling confidently
through pulsating vastnesses
of crab nebulas and black holes.

Dazzling illuminations hang suspended
trapped in festal glory.
An immense galaxy of motion
hanging above the little town.
How splendidly fearful is this sky.
How splendidly fearful the artist
must have been.

The very mysteries of being
seem locked in this canvas.
For those who would seek
look long and hard,
for the measure of infinity is there.
This sky would burst free
from its priceless prison,
and fly above the world
if it could.

Irene Hazell

Summer's Eve

Through the open doors and windows I can hear a deafening noise
There's a mower whining loudly 'cross the way,
And the kid next door is yelling - what a penetrating voice -
While there's six or seven others out to play.

They are shouting, and they're screaming, I suppose they're having
fun?
while the big 'uns bash the small ones on the head,
In the gardens either side a pram is parked to catch the sun,
With the babies yelling fit to wake the dead.

Pigeons sitting on the rooftops, calling loudly 'Who's a fool?'
Blackbirds whistling their defiance from a tree,
And the girl next door plays records - she has just come home from
school-
Overhead some helicopters, two or three.

Across the road a man is tuning up his brand new car,
He has had the engine running for an hour,
While the girl a few doors down the road is yelling to her ma,
That she's going to go upstairs and take a shower.

There are people in the village, campanology's their game,
Wednesday nights they tug the ropes with all their might,
And at weddings they will have a go, it really is a shame
That instead of tunes, the bells just seem to fight!

All the moggies in the road meet in our garden every night,
Cat-a-wauling, hissing, meowing out of key,
'til my 'better half' chucks out a boot to give those mogs a fright,
And he looks so wild he even frightens me!

Summer nights are ruined by noise - oh how I long for winters' quiet,
(I don't mind the howling winds and lashing rain)
If it keeps the kids indoors, and all the mowers out of sight
Then I'll really welcome winter back again.

Joyce Barnard

Geriatric Ward

'Come on, come on. Won't somebody help me, please?'
The plea is constant, unremitting,
It strains our pity with its low insistence.
'Come on, come on. Won't somebody help me? Please'

Twisted hands reach out, clawing at air
The frail body struggles to sit briefly upright,
Slumps back, head lolling, limbs contorted.
'Come on, come on. Won't somebody help me, please'.

The mouth gapes and we post food into it,
The jaws chew ponderously, dribbling little morsels down the chin,
A tongue appears and greedily reclaims them,
Briefly there is silence with the effort of eating...

We wash the thin old baby and there is no struggle
Only a little trembling of the wasted limbs.
There is no spark in the half shut eye.
It is hard to know if this is sleep or waking.
If sleeping, are there dreams?

'Come on, come on. Won't somebody help me, please?'

That cry so weary on the ears is the cry of the lost soul
Trapped in inferno. Striving for heaven, but endlessly cast down.
It is the cry of the soul fettered in a sick body
In a world no longer homely or significant.
It is the frantic, helpless, beating on the bars
Of a caged bird longing to be free.
It confronts us horribly with our own mortality.

I stroke her palm. Her fingers close round mine
Suddenly, out of the pit a familiar voice, but changed, is speaking,
'My, my your hands are warm, my dear.'
M Patrick

157

O' Death

O' death this is your sting, the loneliness that
you bring, to all of us who are left behind, to
have to shed these tears and bear this pain
and know on earth we will not see our loved
ones again.

The loneliness we have to bear, the empty
room, the empty chair, the empty bed, when
we go there.

We talk and there is no reply and we
think O why, O why. Why we know we have to
try and live on, but this is hard, with our
loved ones gone.

Life is not the same it cannot be,
we just have to wait for our Eternity
Death you cannot win the more life you
take the more life begins.

H W Walder

158

Too Generous With My Love

Too generous with my love;
I heaped it up,
I hoarded it for you.
Impassioned, overwhelming, sure,
So ignorant, my love.
And, like an ill-balanced column of coins
It lurched and swayed,
Then, in a sickening golden rush,
Fell; scattering apart its spurned and futile wealth.

Now, as I crawl away,
Bruised and nauseous,
Too shocked to grieve,
Other selfish, greedy hands
Still scrabble for the
Hollowed coins,
To claim the worthless fragments
As their own.

Alison Thirza

Contentment

If I can find a beauty
In a rain-washed day,
If I can feel excitement
In the wind's rough play.
And if I find contentment
In the sun's warm smile.
Surely these are things
To make life worthwhile!

If I can find a quiet joy
In everything I do.
If all the finer things in life
To me, are simple, too!
And if the hand of friendship
Is there for all to see.
Am I a fool to be content
With such felicity!

Iris Allingham

In the City

Cardboard boxes in the city
Housing suffering and shame
Needing helping hand not pity
Seeking hope but all in vain
City folk in cardboard boxes
Its the only home they know
Empty hearts and empty pockets
No where else for them to go
Trying hard to break the circle
Lifting feet up off the ground
Searching for elusive ladder
That is no where to be found
It's a never ending battle
Victory can not be won
Until some body beats the system
Finding home's for every one.

Margaret Thompson

A Concoction of Smells

Newly tarred roads
Manure in loads.

Hot spiced vinegar
Pickled onions in a jar.

Lemon zest grated
Curry flavour overrated.

Joint of meat roasting
Slice of bread toasting.

Oak logs burning
Roast chestnuts turning.

A freshly mown lawn
Coffee aroma drawn.

Washing drying on the line
Fresh sage, mint and thyme.

Honeysuckle heaven sent
Sweetpeas scent, delightment.

Stephanie Ames

Drugs

How sorry I am now
That I didn't listen to my mum.
All I wanted to do
Was go out and have some fun.

How I wish with all my heart
I had not partied so much,
So then those evil drugs
I might never have even touched.

I wanted to be like the others
So I thought I'd have just one puff.
It was only 'grass' after all
I'd never use the 'hard stuff'!

That's what I thought then,
That's how it all started
But now I am addicted
And my family are broken hearted.

It's heroin and cocaine now
That get me on a high.
These drugs are more expensive
And bled my bank account dry.

I've sold all my possessions
And half of my family's too.
If I can't get more dope
I don't know quite what I'll do.

I'm sleeping with fellows for money.
I'm in the lowest of all trades.
I know that I am pregnant
And am now, dying of AIDS.
Karen Lucy Bianchi

The French Sensation

Sun streaked, tree-lined roads stretching long into the distance.
Bleached bundles of hay adorning roadside fields with chateaux
                                    sprinkled carelessly as backdrops.
Old farm houses, apparently derelict, clucking to life as hens escape
                                                    onto the road.
Small, dark hotels with floral wallpaper and creaking floors revealing
Delightful courtyards where one can dine leisurely when chef has
                                        performed his magic.
Modest bedrooms complete with clothed table, chair and the odd
mosquito which has solved the maze of the shutters.
The clanking of petanques in the square of even the most modest
                                                            town.
Groups of weathered old men gathering for serious talk at corners.
Quiet evening streets, only occasionally releasing glimmers of light
                                        from shuttered houses.
Croissants, coffee and strong 'chocolat' signalling early mornings.
Days punctuated with delicious aromas of repasts unrivalled in
                                        culinary excellence.
Calm, broad river gliding past the shimmering chateaux of the Loire.
Vines hung ripe with grapes and a thousand chances to sip the best at
                                        'caves' along the route.
Red, pantiled roofs guiding the way South.
Memorable scents of lavender, luring one down from the Alps to
                                        perfumed Grasse.
Corner cafes, vivid parasols, palm trees and the chattering of a
                language which seems to move just a little too quickly...
The Cote D'Azur - bustling with life, bursting with colour, blanched
with the sun - taking one's breath away.
Bronzed bodies on burning beaches of white sand.
Expensive couture, chic boutiques and swimwear of the briefest
                                                            kind.
Yachts we only dream of, dressed in splendour as costumed waiters
                                serve cocktails on the upper deck.
Tooting car horns impatient to reach some romantic destination.

164

Fresh seafood to fascinate the gourmet and fromage to tempt the
dullest palate.
Speciality pastries, too perfect to eat
Colourful vegetables and herbs enticing the visitor to linger in noisy
markets.
Aspiring Lautrecs lining the streets with the fruits of their labours.
Spectacles, tastes, perfumes combining to provide the French
sensation.
This is the France I love bountiful, beautiful, blissful.

Hilary J Messeter

Starlings

Summoned by outposted scout
Spotting all the food put out,
Nigh forty, flying, flashy, loud,
From all sides descend, a cloud
Of iridescent blue, black, green,
In polka-dotted feathered sheen.

Wing flapping, beak stabbing, eager lot,
Their pecking order not forgot,
The table fill to overflow,
While others strut the lawn below,
Impudent, impatient to be among
The quarrelsome, hoyden, upper throng.

The feast begins and, manners-shy,
Viands in all directions fly.
Hierarchy dissolves in such distortion
For each to snatch the other's portion.
The banquet soon becomes a brawl,
A fluttering, frenzied, free-for-all.

The repast cleared, some take a bath,
The water splashed across the path.
They drink, they bathe, they argue still,
Contending with each other, till
At someone's bidding off they fly,
Some other venue next to try.

Comic, ribald, ruffian crew,
To their tribe allegiant, true,
Love them, dislike them, as one may,
To the garden day by day
They bring an entertainment there,
A cameo of life to share.
W J Moore

Epitaph or Secret Drinker

Sitting in my armchair a bottle by my side
I haven't any more to lose since I lost my pride.

My wife has said goodbye to me, another
man she will choose, everything I have lost
through the demon booze.

No one wants to know me, so I was cast
aside, I took with me my bottle and in my room
I'd hide.

I drank to drown my sorrow's till this conclusion
I had come, the more I drank to drown them
the better swimmers they become.

I drank in moderation until it got a hold,
while getting short of money my possessions I
have sold.

No shoes on my feet no hat upon my head,
Just a wooden overcoat, as you can see I'm
dead.

As you are reading this I hope that you can
see, I died at the age of forty-five,
but was 'dead' at thirty three.

I asked for this inscription to be put upon
my tomb, to save all you young people
from meeting an early doom.

Ted M Smith

Tough

I'm tough! Is that what you say
Awaiting the trouble you face today?
All alone, maybe, locked in a cell
One-time friends gone missing as well
A list of charges, not all mine,
Being heard in court, today, sometime
Of fraud, extortion, rape or stealing
Adultery, drugs, and excess drinking.
Other wrongs may spring to mind
That seem enticing to mankind
And, how can I get out of debt?
Jesus looked on Jerusalem, and wept...

Bringing a halt to an execution,
Jesus said, as she stood alone
'Let the one without sin,
Cast the first stone.'
Tough? Yes? He, who faced such angry crowd,
'Father, forgive them, they know not
What they do.' Our Lord, said this,
As they nailed him to a crucifix.
I never knew I meant that much, to Him,
When lost and blind to my own sin.
Like to meet this friend? Is your path rough?
He isn't *deaf,* but staunch, and tough.

Frances Ellen Woodfield-Readdie

168

Harvest

Just down the valley from yesterday's tears,
we sit in the kitchen describing our fears
over the bird and under the stag
fetching up sorrows from an open bag.
Out in the fields the round bales stand
ready to roll and flatten the land.
Her hands for zips and buttons are fumbling,
soon on her bed our forms will be tumbling.

The seduction is serious but the encounter's too late.
Is it quite fair to put in the Tate
a model of lust that's stuffed full of brushes?
Between our bodies absurdity rushes
ready to show with wicked precision
how much is chance, how little decision.

Charles Kaye

Airport

The waft of coffee and sweaty bodies
Sticking to safari shirts,
Boys slither on their bellies
Looking up ladies skirts.
A right little horror sits, sulking and pulling faces
And his T-shirt over his knees, which reads,
'I've been to the London Dungeons',
And the father looking on with an evil glare,
Wishing to God he'd left him there.
Japanese tourists move in neat packs,
Bags full of souvenirs, union Jacks,
Cameras bouncing and small ruck sacks,
As they dash for their flight back home.
An old man squints behind glasses
Staring at the screen up above,
Patting his wife and pointing,
'Can't make nowt out of that love'.
Heads appear on ascending stairs
To white, polished floors and cushioned chairs
And more people:
Tired men carrying heavy cases
With furrowed brows and beetroot faces,
A rough looking Scotsman screaming and shouting,
While nuns discuss a Lourdes outing,
Rose cheeked Italians beginning to cry
As they kiss and hug their loved ones goodbye,
Cherry nosed Paddies sitting in the bar
Gulping down jar after jar,
And oversized Americans feeding their faces
In monotone voices discuss different places they've been to.

Susan Lafferty

The Aegian Isle of Rupert Brooke

Far up the narrow little path
Where poppies and the ilex laugh,
By olive trees that weep and moan
There lies the grave of one well known.

For he who loved England much,
So dear to him his thoughts were such
That should he in a strange land die
A part of England there would lie.

The blue-green waters of the seas
Surround the isle where olive trees
Bear gnarled branches black and grey,
Which flower and fruit eternally.

Just see the tortoise play, and oh!
How sweet the sage blooms now, I know!
For yet this rock garden of flowers
Is the most beautiful of bowers!

So on this isle of marble white
They buried him one April night,
The moon against the mountains shone,
The flowers showed where he had gone.

This paradise, this olive-grove,
Where scents of mint and thyme are wove,
Could I but know the reason why
A poet young should have to die?

Elizabeth Dove

171

Over Here

In the nineteen forties,
In the second world war;
The Yanks and Canadians
Were drafted over here.

With the Yanks the girls had fun,
On the street corners chewing gum,
Hank and Jerry, Bud and Don,
Buying them Pimms No.1

They flirted with all the girls,
Every night they had their twirls,
At their camp dances they danced non-stop,
The quick step, jive and military two-step.

There was lots of romance in the air,
Those handsome hunks were over here;
Bubble gum and Coco-cola,
Cigarettes; Camel and Lucky Strike,
They puffed away from morn till night.

They shared their chocolates and their cigs,
Oh, life was just one long whizz;
From clothes coupons carefully saved,
The girls bought dresses on which they raved,
Remember, these were rationing days.

Stepping out almost every night,
Through the wartime blackout;
Even Clark Gable was over here,
But to see him, we couldn't get near.

Oh boy, did they have fun;
Knocking back the gin and rum;
Our British lads got very shirty,
And on the walls was the graffiti;
Yanks go home', said the bold text,
You're overpaid and oversexed.

Marian Brodie

Perfect Love

I watch her sleeping and my heart is full
Of affection and wonder that she chose me;
The bonding has strengthened since she moved in
And our joy is intense as we knew it would be.

On the sofa relaxing during long winter evenings,
Curled up together, her head on my chest,
Words are not needed to express our feelings,
Content with each other, at peace and at rest.

With perceptive green eyes looking into my face
She senses my moods without anything said,
Inviting me to involve her, she goes on to persuade
Me to talk of my feelings - so problems are shared.

During long lie-ins we meld together,
I stroke down her back, either side of her spine,
She responds in kind with gentle sounds of pleasure,
Her body outstretched, entwined with mine.

I would never believe this could happen to me,
The love and the friendship, maturing with time;
To come home to someone, her welcome to see,
So perfect, so sensuous - and every inch feline.

J L Service

Reunion

In her hand she held a token
A worn out souvenir
Of a heart that once was broken
And a love she held so dear
beside her lay the picture of
A young man strong and sure
He was her one and only love
Sent away to war
She never saw her love again
He never came back home
The rest of her life was spent in pain
And all alone
And now her sad life is through
Alone she lived, and died
Loving the young man who
Was in the picture by her side
She lay there, lifeless and still
And I felt so sad for a while
I cried for her broken heart until
On her face, I saw, a smile
She lived without a smile or laugh
It seemed strange that now she should
I looked up at the photograph
And understood
The young man stood brave and dutiful
His smile was bright and wide
And she looked so very beautiful
The young girl by his side

Lynda Bailey

175

Waterwheel

Turn, turn waterwheel
You magical man made thing
Swirl back the echos of childhood...
Six years old stands eyes widening to your spellbinding
The river is a sun kissed quiver of restless water

You turned and churned, churned and turned
You magical man made thing.

Sounds of wash and gush, muffle and throb and creak
of aged wood
Smells of damp and pools of murky darkness
sends imagination soaring
Six years old face sprayed wet with the sweat
of your great wooden brow whilst the day bides
in a static sweetness of a child's summer wonder

You churned and turned, turned and churned
You magical man made thing.

The days buzzed with jewelled damsel flies
glinting like iridescent helicopters in dust
dancing shafts of sunlight
Come the soft purple pluge of nightfall the
trees will nod in sleepy silhouette to your
splish splosh lullaby
Moonlight softly fingers silver shadows to
sooth your unceasing toil

You turned and churned, churned and turned
You magical man made thing

Turn, turn waterwheel
You magical man made thing.
Barbara Lane

176

Chiming of Bells

Listen as the chimes wallow then all eager boil again
And like the sea they grandious patterns make
Linking trebles rise and fall like a silver chain
While the great bass 'drang' and 'drong' in their wake.

Plunging and clashing down mighty walls of stone
Clanging tenors lace through this sabbath sound
Loud peels disturb the peace of each ancient bone
Buried beneath this cruciform of holy ground.

Then pervading all space from altar vault and nave
This joyous sound surges all restless to be free
And hangs as if upon a vibrant wave
To plunge once more in clanging harmony.

Kenneth Child

The Decline of a Village (Society?)

Over twenty six years have gone by.
Since we moved from town to St John's Lye.
A young family then, with dreams, and full of hope.
On our own at last, and learning to cope.

People cared about others then.
Now it's number one, not them.
The grass in front no longer there.
A place to park! they don't care.

The village shops are no more.
Driven out by a bigger store.
Open early morn till late at night.
Even Christmas day, can that be right?

When the evenings are fine, a rowdy rabble.
Shouting, swearing, a constant babel.
The local youth, they like to congregate.
The noise from motor bikes, it's getting late!

Early dreams are now a nightmare.
People today, just don't care.
Unable to move, we are here to stay.
Will things improve? We can only pray.

Patricia Bannister

Celandines

I notice dear flower at noon
How your myriad faces bloom
As they glisten and shine yellow and bright
At the welcoming sun making its flight

I notice dear flower at dawn
As I awake to greet the morn
How your petals are closed and you are at rest
You may be sure I am impressed

Little creature, living flower
Dwelling within your heart-shaped bower
A miracle has made you perfect and pure
Entering the world in March so raw

Nature's herald, calling Springtime's arrival
Shiny and yellow, damp with dew
Sweet celandine, dear celandine
We take our cue from you

Margaret Clare

The Rock

Timeless,
Ever present,
Solid as a rock,
Even in absence,
You have presence.

Waves thrash and roar,
White fists beat upon my door,
Then past the tempest I can see,
The Lighthouse Keeper beckoning me,
To sanctuary.

Riding the waves,
Taking up the oars,
The light guides me,
With an inner certainty,
Of not being drowned,
This time around.

The Lighthouse Keeper, Guardian of light,
Can be called upon, in the dead of night,
Watching over, eternally there,
He aids me in my black despair.

Bernadette Geraghty

Friend of My Youth

Oh! Friend of my youth
I remember the good times we had.
You cared for me
You were good to me.
But I said farewell to you
At the crossroads of my life.
Oh! Friend of my youth
I remember you with love.

It was you who walked me home
From my first dance.
It was you who took me sailing
Across the bay.
And we parted one evening
On the quay.
You went your way
And I went mine.
Oh! Friend of my youth
I remember you with love.

It was with you I spent my carefree
Summer days of yesteryear.
It was with you I first saw
A shooting star.
Oh! Friend of my youth
I remember you with love.

Barbara Geraghty

181

The Oldest Magic

From the hips of dancing partners
Moving slowly
Like thieves on this night
Stealing this moment from each other
We walked barefoot through fields ablaze
A carpet of roses and rubies
Evoking a ritual of things we hold passionate
Spiritual penalties may be incurred
As we are draped and woven
Into this crimson tapestry
As the sounds that danced in their mirth
Now gently subside
The stillness beckons us to move closer
Evening whispers in soft tongues
For this is the oldest magic

Michael Turton

Full Circle

Oh dear, oh dear, I'm getting old.
Can't stand the heat, but feel the cold.
The stairs steeper every day
There's not a thing I'll throw away.
The police aren't looking younger now
They're not around, nowhere, nohow!

If I go out and take a walk
I'll pat a dog, then stop to talk.
I shop a bit, get this and that,
A shop's a place where you can chat.
I lock my door when I'm inside
If salesmen call I sometimes hide.

I tend my garden when I'm fit
Get out my deckchair, sit and knit.
My neighbours' cat sits on the wall,
But he ignores me when I call.
My grandchildren live far away,
But 'praps one day they'll come and stay.

I always keep a biscuit tin
You never know who might pop in.
My 'telly's' sometimes on he blink,
But never mind, I sit and think.
I listen to 'The Archers', too,
There's always something you can do.

I've got no time for those who moan
It's sometimes nice to live alone.
At least that's what I always say.
I'll not be beaten there's no way!
I'm getting older every day,
But so are you, so that's fair play.
Joan Newman

The Trees Infernal Reaching For Times Eternal Teaching

And a spiteful appletree
grew from evil happily
with its roots in decay
and its fruits in array,
dismay was its longing
living, killing then dying.

Dead and suffering penitence
for its deeds of evil opulence
sharing in the bearing boughs
all the suffering of its cause,
thus the seed was crushed
perpetually into deaths dust.

But all things have a living end
and times patient creation and
faithful regeneration testify truth -
that seeds all grow is proof,
therefore life is the seed of itself
so it grew its true appletree self.

The bark bending in supple strength
joyful growth oath lauded in length
its platinum reflection of inside
core spent and spoken outside,
turning to justice its hunger
for a life stronger and longer

If a seed does usurp greed
then unhappiness becomes its need
but if instead from its bed
it gratefully rises with a happy head
a glowing future shall you see
in the presents living fruitfully.

William Acciu

Broken Dream - Reawakening

Like a ripe fruit, waiting to be picked;
Like an autumn-golden leaf,
    Fluttering in a silk-soft breeze,
    Ready to be enticed from the tree,
My body quivers in anticipation
    Of the touch of hands so gentle, so tantalising,
    That they brush my skin as softly as a whisper.

Every nerve and muscle taut with expectation.
Motionless now; even breath is stilled.
Awaiting the sun-burst of feeling that the first touch promises.

No censorious thoughts intrude here.
Imagining the exquisite sensation of a caress.
Skin touching skin,
Lazily, unhurried, because time has tiptoed away, smiling softly,
    Leaving only peace and pleasure, languid loving.

Revelling in the joy given and received
    In those loving, caring touches.
Heart leaping and laughing with happiness
    At the release of long-forgotten feelings.
Amazed at the new-found knowledge that my body does not disgust,
    But is loved for itself, with all its faults,
    For in this oasis of suspended time,
    The imperfect is perfect.
Filled with awe at the strength and certainty that this loving gives.

And then, sadness at knowing it is only a dream,
  And I must wake and leave it unfinished,
  With a sense of loss, for feelings still dormant,
  Still undisturbed.

But from dreams come hopes,
  And today's hopes may become tomorrow's reality.

Kathryn Ramsay

Intercity

Locked inside a tube
of modern technology
the luminous tubed lighting
and rows of orange/grey seats
rush through the luscious
green and brown patched landscape,
so fresh and vital in a modern world.
The spaces as yet left
alone by man and his
insistence on progress.
Industrialization; houses,
factories, shops.
The spaces left which we
so often forget in our anger
at the destruction of natures work.
The spaces which can fill us
with hope: hope that it is
not too late to save our world.
And yet, these views are seen
from inside a tube
of modern technology.

Barley Dellaway

To the Spirit of Poetry

You passed me in the silent night,
Quiet as the owlets silken flight
Beneath the trees at half light
When one by one the stars are lit.

Soft your touch as thistle-down,
along the little breezes blown,
Seeking in the compassionate earth
A womb, to await the hour of birth.

So quiet you passed and gone so soon,
(A wisp of cloud across the moon)
I had but time to hear you sigh
In the trees as you wing'ed by.

Just time to know your presence there
And catch the fragrance of your hair,
Then to stand in the night alone
And watch where one great star shone.

Far and far my spirit streaming
To your star, so richly gleaming,
A word to relish from your song,
To fail and fall to depths headlong.

Secretly now I watch the star,
Furtive and desolate from afar,
Your presence never known to me
As alone I wait beneath the tree.

From the arching heavens thrust,
My soul a note of dancing dust,
Bitter and grey about your feet,
My dreams all shattered in defeat.
Maurice Cyril Ricks

Dreaming Reality

I can feel your heart
Beating against my chest
You sleep now, soundly.
I stroke your hair,
Caress each pore of your
Silk-like skin and
Watch you dream.
'Til I too slip silently into
That darkened place.
Where I dream of moonlit shores
And moulded sands.
There I stay 'til dawn,
Holding you close against my skin.
No-one can perceive this love of ours
It is un-denied and timeless
And stretches far beyond this world.
For all to see, we wander alone
Through each day.
But in our minds our hearts are joined.
A cloud passes by,
Solitary, lonesome and I know
You can see it too.
I think of you and what you're doing and
I wait patiently until
The days' toils are over
And I can return.
When our bodies will cling
And words will flow and
My love, once again,
I can show you.

Kevin Spicer

Picaroon

Did he know they called him 'Picaroon'
And would he really care, or be glad
That at last he'd been noticed,
'On the map', a social label,
A certain type of rogue,
A yob, a thief, a bloody nuisance,
They all sounded good to him.

'Don't matter if I'm caught'
He thought in someone elses car,
'I'm too young to go to jail,
Just claim stupidity and youth,
And if I'm lucky they'll put me on
A car maintenance course
For telling the truth'.

So he carried on the game,
Everyone knew his ways and haunts
And some came out to watch him
On Friday nights, in a stolen car
But he didn't go far, not enough
To be stopped by the police
And he never dreamt he'd kill.

Lights off, night, a screaming run,
A stunt to pull for everyone,
With his pals all squeezed in front and back,
Fighting, shrieking, popping, freaking,
Mooning, cooing, wooing, dreaming,
The child ran out, the screech, the silence,
No car course came his way.

He knew they called him Picaroon
But he didn't understand.

Michael Webster

191

Yvonne Alone, Formerly Darling

'I am: yet what I am none cares or knows,
perhaps, then, I am not,'

Yvonne, now lonely, reasoned.

And fearful of such spidery thought,
sought refuge, first in food,

and later, in flight to a parfumerie,
and was, temporarily.

Once again, at home, alone,

Yvonne held up the mirror, which,
having no sense of smell, lied, wickedly.

'If no-one else but a rose bush knows
how good mud feels between one's toes,

I shall exist like a plant,' she said.
So prepared her return to the earth.

And very little care hath she,
yet, still, existing painfully,
she sings: 'how cold my toes, tiddely pom, are growing.'

(Thanks to Metheun Childrens Books, for permission to use extracts
from 'The House At Pooh Corner' by A A Milne)
Linda Young

The Third World

He's ten years old, his world is Third
The only one he's known
There are other worlds, so he's been told
With riches all their own.

His world beneath the burning sun
The chilling sand his bed
He's starving, surely it's the right
That simple souls be fed

His mother, in a far off day
Heard of a God that's kind
But they, within this awful plight,
Are very hard to find.

He often sees his brothers die
There's sadness in a way,
soon he learns more share is his
To survive another day.

for miles and miles he walks and seeks
A place to call his home,
He hears that help is on the way
No more has he to roam.

There are many others in despair
Thro' bars, no hope they see
But oh! the pain that hunger brings
Otherwise he's free.

Food and help is getting near
thank those who see the need,
May compassion spread through all the world
None starve for others greed.

Let everyone be free.

Ida Chaney

The Place

There are beasts on the Masai Mara.'
Wild things that haunt the night, that stalk the maimed,
That feed on the crippled, the lost and lame.
Creatures without conscience
And fiends of cold pity
That prey to a frightful litany
Of lust and hate.

And at one place on the scorched arid plain
They give full rein to orgies of cruelty and pain.
At a place that bears mute testament still
To their relish of the hellish tortures they inflict
Under the moon's tearing horn
Before skulking like hyena shadows
Into the dawn.

A place to which only the vultures can lead you;
To where the scattered, shattered sun scarred skulls
Eternally accuse, casting hollow-eyed glares
At the atrocities emblazoned on the burning air.
A place that shimmers like shivering flesh,
Where the sand weaves its way like wisps of honey coloured hair.
A place where the stones are soaked with screams,
Where the horror still hangs on the winds' hot breath;
this place where Julie Ward
Died her long, lingering
And lonely death.

Richard Toogood

Old Man of the Beach

He comes at night from moonlit beach
Dressed in rags no shoes on feet
And as the night falls on your town
He spreads his web of sleep around

Alone and old he casts a gaze
To every room on every face
And if you're not in bed he knows
The good from bad - it always shows

That strange old man with battered feet
Owns a spell - the gift of sleep
If he comes and you're not there
He'll turn your dreams into nightmares

Then never more would you rest
Because you were no longer blessed
But he always wants to find you there
Safe in bed, he's a friend that cares

This wisened man will smile on you
And send you dreams good and true
So be sure to pull the covers tight
When you go to bed tonight!

For the children that sleep - and the ones that don't!

Simon Parker

Sanctuary

I need a place to escape to.
A mental idea brought to reality.
Somewhere where I close my eyes
And gentle duvets surround me.
Mellow sounds caress my ears,
While feathers are so comforting.
Everything moves in slow motion.
No speed, no jolt and no rushing.

The lights are dim so unpretentious.
They only see my body - naked,
That lies within my peaceful cocoon
The walls that keep out those non-placid.
Walls are floors and other things.
Weightlessness, like in most dreams
Warm, cool sunshine bringing bliss.
Everything is what it seems.

I need no food, I need no water
Wants just pass me by.
This sanctimonious solitude
I see in my minds eye.
Give me time and lots of pleasure
Let me stay where I won't weep

- I want to live in sanctuary
- I want to live there permanently

I need, I need continuous sleep.

Nicola Bovell

January Afternoon

Houses, eyes closed, slumber in the grey air.
Dispirited smoke tumbles down roofs,
(Offending nostrils).
Someone, small, grey head down hurries past.
Trees motionless.

Cars swish by on wet roads.
Unseen plane momentarily shakes the sleeping air
And sodium streetlights wink awake to welcome evening;
The heavy afternoon waits.

Cream and red bus,
Lighted friendly misted windows,
Children calling friends.
Women - Tesco bags and headscarves;
And somewhere a blackbird sings.

Rosemary Osborne

Chinese Inspiration

The day has stretched ahead,
Filling me slowly and yet creative thoughts
Come through, so that I forget my
Loneliness.

Chinese silk, I release tension
Through this painting; Light pinks
And hues of delicate blue
So that I no longer relieve

Headaches perhaps, but boredom.
The flowers seemed like vervain -
Terrain grown bold now and cold , grey
Hips of sea just said to me,
Contrasts.

We must continue, on silk, the paper
Slows brush. Tension grows as I work
Push tip and flow and rush through
Moments of Timorousness
To silence.

Ellinor Gordon Lennox

A Dream for All Seasons

The years have slipped passed almost unnoticed.
Recent meetings have stirred my hearts desire,
Love's edge is sharp, untouched by time.
The thaw of our separation has begun.

Fate has delivered you the gift of new life!
His smile is the Spring of our courting time.
The end of your strife is what I seek,
The requital of my love is within reach.

The Summer of our love will be long and warm,
The sweetness of your kiss will be my elixir.
The waters of my love run deep and cool
And will quench your thirst for peace and joy.

The heat of my passion shall warm us through
The blissful Autumn of our life together.
And when life's leaves have paled and yellowed,
Death's Winter of separation shall surely be short.

When in heaven, we are again together,
These seasons of love will be but a dream,
For the reign of our love will be forever,
Through time and space and thereon, after.

If this, my dream, you do not share,
Then Winter's chill will freeze my love
And there, preserved, it will stay forever,
Until, once more, it's stirred and warmed.

So come sweet love and claim my soul,
Bathe in the pool of love which I hold.
No fire can shake the grip of my Winter's cold,
Save the kiss of your love reaching my heart.

Edward Thackeray

Everybody's Lovely When They Smile

Faces have expressions,
of each and every kind,
and sometimes those expressions,
can say what's on your mind.

If you're feeling troubled,
but are hiding the bad way,
People will still notice,
by what expressions say.

Faces that have glamour,
can show a kind of style,
but any face is lovely,
when it bears a smile,

It's a sign of happiness,
a truly lovely thing,
to see somebody's face,
when it is smiling.

No matter what you look like,
whatever is your style,
just remember everybody's
lovely when they smile!

Jackie Figg

Past and Present

How quietly the seconds slip away.
Furtively, wary of being caught.
And soon it will be another day,
And nothing to show for the time that passed.
How short is a lifetime!
How easily it drifts away.
A swiftly disentangled line
That took so long to weave.
A misty, distant memory
Fades further in the depths of time,
And presences of lives to be
Begin to focus and solidify.
How tenuous the link 'twixt then and now,
The line that holds the past!
The strokes on paper that endow
The knowledge we have gained.
And who, then, will remember you?
What gifts have you bestowed?
What thoughts have you shown to be true?
What mysteries unfurled?
And oh, so many pass away,
A fleeting breath of life.
And nothing left of them to say
'This is what I have achieved.'
And oh, so few that leave behind
Ideas, and things of beauty.
And these the only threads that bind
Past and present resolutely.

Jane L Dards

M25

Enter the chaos
between two to thirty-one,
ride the circle in search of services
and junction one.

Southbound headlights,
blue signs, whitelines, lane closures, cones
Northbound tail lights;
It's all much the same.

Four lanes, soon
talk of eight?
A bypass for a bypass
In the planners head.

Suburban ring road for a capitol of lights
on the maps a maze of yellows and blues,
the weekends spent in Reigate, Staines, Leatherhead of Slough,
back to work on Monday and the traffic queues...

Adrian Caradine

Ethna: 1938-1977

Nuns are there that without the convent walls
Conduct their lives, and thou wert one of those,
Who walked within the mind's sad cloistered halls,
Wearing its sober habit of repose.
And nuns there are of other sort again,
Whose calling is of even costlier kind,
Whose lot it is throughout the world in vain
To seek a dwelling-place and nowhere find:
Nuns of select, devoted sisterhood,
Who need no bells to summon them to prayers:
No greater rule or lesser ever could
Inspire a sterner discipline than theirs.
As sisters we two walked a little space;
Now one of us has found her resting-place.

Carole T O'Driscoll

The Last Wolf*

Mateless, gaunt, she printed long ago
Faint epitaph of footmarks on the snow.

Hunted lone through final years of dread,
Stiffened lies at last the last wolf, dead.
Tears have grooved her muzzle, tawny-grey,
In seeming sorrow at this wasteful day,
And ants parade the dry and shrunken dugs,
Nurture once for playful growing cubs.
The shepherd is well pleased, his fleecy dams
May safely graze and raise their many lambs:
Hardly worth removal of that skin -
Its bloody coat so torn and patchy thin!

The evening ends with jubilance and jeers;
But one youth feels, alone of all his peers,
The pity of those glazed yet flowing eyes,
And nightfall is pervaded by his sighs:
No more might canny prick-eared pack be spied
Loping distant glen, or mountainside.
Today with due respect he would conserve
Remaining groups to manage, and observe
An excellence of leadership and law
He cannot in his deepest heart deplore.

Mateless, gaunt, she printed long ago
Faint epitaph of footmarks on the snow.

*Killed in Scotland 1743

Diana Dykes

205

The Country Lane

Winding it goes, the lane near the village
that follows the ancient track;
High the hedges on either hand,
shawled with roses, guardian stand,
and on the steep, green banks below
Campion and Stitchwort grow,
and bees about their business go.

Shady it winds, the trees arching over,
down to the old stone bridge, -
Distant the shout of a child at play,
or a tractor chugging its dusty way,
all else is Peace in the scented air, -
a tiny splash shows that Ratty's there
where the water washes its grass-green hair.

But they'll widen the lane that runs near the village,
the Planning and Shouting is through.
Martian machines will munch and maul
and pile the spoil, so stark, so tall,
then the road will run through in a straight, broad band,
and a Concrete bridge will proudly stand
and laud it over the crying land.

'Oh! the new road's fine' the commuters say,
'It saves at least twenty minutes each day!'
But Peace has gone, and Ratty won't play,
and I walk no more that ancient way.

Jeanette Marmion

Track Marks

Sun
and wind
and rain
have etched your face.

More lines than
the London Underground
you told me
once.

Each track
tells a story
when a smile
spills
in gentle rivulets
from around
your eyes.
I'd call them laughter lines
if you'd let me

but you always said
nothing
could be that
funny.

Ken Jones

The Bread Queue

It was dark, very early,
The queues were there.
It was snowing hard.
Feet shuffled in the cold.
The shop was dark
Not yet open.
There was the hope
Bread would come
Warm from the oven.
Already they had waited
Hours in the freezing snow.
Every day the queues began,
Early - long before the day.
the angry young,
The patient old.
They were all there
Waiting in the Moscow snow.

Margery Horwood

The Morning Horse

The morning horse gallops out of her dream,
Head tossed, mane flying, the drumming of hooves,
Across the muddy field and cold-heart stream.

The girl rides well in sleep eyes seen,
Twisted sheets as reins; in iron-bright shoes,
The morning horse gallops out of her dream.

She dreams of plaited tails and grooming clean,
A shying step and a voice that soothes,
Across the muddy field and cold-heart stream.

Long hours work at bit and rolled eyes mean,
Red, shame-faced words as quickened tempers lose,
The morning horse gallops out of her dream.

A cheek caressed, the soft muzzle's sheen,
The hugs are strong, the pillow's only use;
Across the muddy field and cold-heart stream.

Across the style of sleep and day between,
The stables gone and there's only backyard views,
The morning horse gallops out of her dream,
Across the muddy field and cold-heart stream.

D J Davies

Ant

He comes into my kitchen, a black speck,
Hurrying in circular, crepuscular motion.
Is there a heart in that small body?
Blood in his veins?
Sexless, he spends his life in selfless devotion,
Eyes, nose, and antennae constantly seeking
To satisfy the needs of all his kin.

And I must kill him
For, if I let him go,
He'll bring his family to raid my cupboard,
Invade my pot of honey.

When he is no more than a dry, black stain,
Hair-like legs crushed and armoured body splintered,
Will he be missed?
One less attendant upon the queen,
Pupae neglected, shrivelled in their cells.
Or will his place be taken by a hundred more,
Tunnelling beneath my floor, to build an empire,
Careless of sun and sky until the day
They lead their empress into light and air,
To spread her wings for one short marriage flight?

My ant will not return to weave his mystic dance,
Leading an army to my precious store.
One firm footstep will keep me safe
And yet .... I hesitate
And let him run.

Adele Misselbrook

Untitled

The dog is in, the cats gone out
the budgies flown away
oh well, here we go
it's the start of another day
I've dropped an egg and burnt the toast
the kids are late for school
oh my, how time flies
I'm due at the local pool
once again back safely home
the kids are out at play
oh no there goes the phone
now what am I going to say
I don't have time, I really must go
my dinner's about to cook
see you then, please ring again
as I dash to the cooker and look
the dinner is ruined, burnt to a crisp
now what am I to do
my husband's due in at any time
does this ever happen to you!

Chris Turner

The Carousel

1.

'How long have we got?' - and it choked me, -
There in the shrouded, white cell;
I needed no answer; received none, -
'I don't know; it's hard to tell.'

Ethereal Chorus

Once more round with the carousel!
'Spare a penny for the guy!'
'The north wind doth blow and we'll have snow'
---'With a pocket full of rye.'

2.

How long have we got? To remember
The ecstacy, laughter and tears.
Blackberry trips, ruddy stained lips
Eternity packed in four years?

Ethereal Chorus

Once more round with the carousel!
'Home again jiggety jog!'
'How many miles to Babylon?'
'Little Tommy Tinker's dog' ---

3.

How long have we got? To remember
Those spine chilling, beach-combing days:
Hot squelching scones, blazing log fires;
Snowdonia lost from our gaze?

Coda

Empty the carousel now,
Silent and chill as the grave,
Blurred and distant the voices.
Only the sway of the swing in the breeze
To recall -
That you were ever there!
How long have we got?
Infinitude!

Mollie Mose

Christmas 1987
(On with the motley)

Behind the paint Grimaldi
makes a Christmas wish;
an audience that will not laugh.
Childhood waits, fragile as the
winter ice beneath the skates
to shatter like a clown's applause.
See reflections of the paint
that stings the eyes
Whiter than the whitest lies
Tighter than the frozen skies
He dances on reflections,
Watches, sees the mirror crack,
clowns must all one day go back
to childhood and it's claws
away from this applause.

Tony Ward

On Iping Bridge

I stood upon the little bridge
At Iping on the Rother
All worries cast upon the wind -
No place was that for bother!

As I was standing there entranced,
I heard a peacock cry:
I turned, and then in wonder saw
The bird ago flaunting by,

And thought the clash of screech and plumes,
Of ugliness and beauty,
Is like the constant fight between
Our pleasure and our duty.

The weeping willow wept for me
That still I'd moralise,
Standing in such a peaceful scene,
So fair before my eyes.

The Rother burbled underneath
The old stone bridge that spanned it,
'The world is lovely: love the world,
Don't try to understand it'.

Good thinking! Loving's easy here
In Sussex in the Spring:
I'll look and feel, and sober thoughts
Into the Rother fling.

Alec Annand

215

At the Moment

'Tell the truth and shame the Devil'
'Honesty is good'
'Always say what's on your mind;
You really know you should'

He is playing games with me
('Two wrongs don't make a right')
But I am scared to speak my truth
Afraid to face a fight

And so I hide the truth from me
From him and friends as well
If patience is its own reward
I'll one day break the spell

Then free from chains of guilt and fear
My freedom safe for me
Truth will return to head and heart
Again I'll honest be

Forgiveness then will come at last
And that will ease the pain
A healing peace shall come to me
And I will love again.

Carol M Harris

The Lonely One

He lays alone in a bed two should share
She's been called to that world beyond compare.
When he thinks of her, and well he might
There's a lump in his throat and it feels very tight
His eyes feel tired and very hot
He knows if he cries he'll cry a lot
And nothing seems right, for she's not there
To extend a hand with loving care.
No icy feet on his any more
No thumps in the night for the occasional snore,
No-one to cuddle when the night is cold
No one to love him when he's grown old.
'Dear God', his heart cries, 'I loved her so,
I shall never understand why she had to go,
It seems when you had a go at your sums
You took one from two and left me the lonely one.'

L Webb

For Worse

I saw him hit her, seven times in all.
Blood flowed from her nose and mouth;
Spattered on the wall.
I watched him kick her, kick her in the head.
He just kept right on kicking her
because of what she'd said.
Some huddled clothes, recoiling on the ground
Whimpering and shrieking
At every snapping sound.
The screams got louder, echoed off the wall.
I still hear shrill and pleading cries
When broken bottles fall.
After the noise stopped, nothing seemed amiss.
Back to the warmth and comfort
of domesticated bliss.
Locked in a kitchen, sobbing, sick with fright
A wife, her role established now...
'till next it's beating night.

Stephen Jones

218

Sea-saw

Where are the wonders of the deep, my friend?
Where are the quilts of coral laid?
Come. Come to where the dolphins roam
And feel yourself and time at one.
Down to the silent, secret, shore.
Below the towering, green-clad, cliff,
Dive in water's air
And know the thrill
Of falling without pain to fear.
Dodge the billowing clouds of fish
That come to see the new creation;
Learn the truth of well-known lore,
And never cease to hearken.

Norrie Thornton

Nag Nag Nag!

He moaned about the button
That from his shirt took flight
Early on a Monday
As it was getting light

He rang about the button
That should be on his shirt
He rang when I was smothered
In oven grease and dirt

He just dropped by at lunchtime
The clock said nearly one
He said 'I thought I'd see Dear
If my button you had done

He called again - believe it
At just on half past two
I said 'Oh blow your button'
I'm, putting on a stew

He rang again that Monday
And I really lost my cool
I screamed 'Forget your button'
The kids are home from school

But I sewed his rotten button
Though it went against the grain
I did that beastly button
So he wouldn't ring again

My charming little sofa
For years had had a sag
I mentioned it on Tuesday
He cried 'Must you always nag!'

M Collins

220

What has he Done?

How could he do it,
Just one man,
Destroy life,
Destroy land,

People have no homes,
Nowhere to go,
No possessions
Nothing, no,

Food is rationed,
Water too,
People are starving,
Are you?

He blew up the oil wells,
Set them to flames,
And the people of Kuwait,
Know who to blame.

He soon came out,
Leaving Kuwait destroyed
And what he had done to the country,
He really enjoyed.

Emma Perkins

Dawn Above Bough Beach

A silver dawn and bird song,
A lake solid, smooth as pearl,
Tall trees that spread dark pools
Across pale fields, and mist
Like primeval steam rising
From the warm crust of an Earth
Still close to its creation,
Untrod, unploughed, unscarred.
Before time could be counted,
No hand to wind the clock,
To wield the knife, the gun,
To grab, despoil, maim, kill.
If this could be our world
So peaceful, clean and still.

Pam Hatcher

Who's Who in Rhyme

I had a leading role it's true,
And tried to do my best for you,
Sometimes things just didn't work out,
That is when people would scream and shout.
All in all it is fair to say,
I liked to do the job my way,
Then a 'Major' change helped me to rest,
But blue is the colour that I like best.

You may remember years ago,
When I starred in a soap you know,
But I packed it in to start anew,
Now singing is the thing I do.
If you can't get my name quite yet,
Then here is a clue that you must get,
My coat of colours will help you out,
So now you should not have a doubt.

Those of you who wish to know.
Will have to sit and watch my show,
My tricks are not to try and deceive,
They are done in a way so as to believe.
The illusions that you may well see
Are mostly done by Deb's and me,
So hold your breath when the tension mounts,
Because to do it right every second counts.

Some people may remember when,
I sang about my friend named Ben,
Song's like this and many others,
Are song's I sang with my four brothers.
I have also made a film or two,
Singing and dancing just for you,
They did not include any muggers or killers,
But for my fans they were certain 'Thrillers'.

Dave Murphy

The Fight

Twisted faces
Red with rage
Bitter words -
From spitting tongues
Nostrils flaring
And eyes glaring
As the first round of battle began.

Emotions have risen to a height
As you sit, with head upright
Beads of sweat burst through your skin
Your heart pounding from within.

Hate exudes from every pore
But you feel there is plenty more
As you hurl abuse to sting
You sense a painful twist within.

Tracey Johnston

Weekend

Weekend - encapsulated,
Contained, on an island,
Crossing the Solent,
Distance sufficient
For island enchantment.
Fields ripening in the sun
Along the ridge,
With trees waving overhead,
The drowning in long grass
To the hum of insects,
Or a skylark's song.
Sea breeze lifting sounds
Of voices from the beach
To meet the strains of love songs
In an empty cafe.
Weekend - encapsulated,
Contained, on an island of the mind.

Ruth Ellacott

The Harbour

It's cold now and nobody's there.
The pointed ears among the tufts
Hark suddenly and show the busy tails.
Distantly looks the house,
Half hidden in the trees
Empty to the boards.
Only the rustle in the tangled hedge
Crossed wet with patterns on the clustered fruit
And the soft wing upon the drooping flower
With all the little life that breeds and teems
Unnoticed.
The jewels that once were roses lose their value.
They lie forlornly on the vacant roof
Which sheltered all the happy summer hours.
There they lived,
Graceful and mute as swans
On the still, circled water.
Nothing was brighter than that air
Nor vivider the colour-painted shapes.
And far beyond
The gladly leaping hills
Enclosed them with the tide.
Confused,
They creep elsewhere to rot their lingering days
They know not when the summer ends
But feel it in their bones.

Jo Appleyard

Horatio

And what of me, my Lord, and what of me?
What kind of life can I have now you've left?
Felicity I'll never meet again
And how'll I ever draw breath but in pain?
King Fortinbras will have no need of me
And what will Denmark's dumbstruck people want?
That I should spend my life recounting yours?
At whose expense? Their own? I have no means.
The only thing to do is write a book,
Be interviewed, a frequent chat-show guest
('How did you feel when your best friend was killed?'),
Make a few quid and found a Hamlet Trust
To fund research into family life
And teach society how to prevent
Such tragedies from happening again ...
No, I'll go back to Wittenburg instead.
Let someone else with greater gifts than mine
Make sense of all this bloodshed. Time won't heal
A single one of all these poisoned wounds
And there's no therapy to help me mourn.
I cannot make a living from the dead,
So of your tale let nothing more be said.

Maurice West

The Sussex Downs

Once more to the sun kissed hills,
The gurgling streams, the silent mills,
Walk with me at cowslip time,
Larks above air like wine,
Forgotten now the dusty towns,
Lost among the magic downs.

There stands Jack with his Jill,
To the west high Duncton Hill,
Now spring breaks through and small lambs bleat,
The cattle at the dewpond meet,
At times the sea mist covers all,
Now seagulls cry 'neath farmyard wall.

Far off Firle beckons me,
As I turn to face the sea,
Southward ebbs the evening tide,
Whispering stay, stay by my side.
As the sun sinks in the west,
The night owl flutters from her nest.

Dusk now brings the harbour light,
All God's creatures face the night,
What sweet mystery our Downs hold,
So many tales as yet untold.

E Knight

In a Nutshell

Awake when others are in bed,
I search old books, I search my head,
I heard it in what someone said,
And you sleep.

There are things I try to arrange,
An image, a place that is strange,
I stare and stare but things don't change,
While you sleep.

I heard a mysterious call,
Flick through a book, stare at the wall,
Is there a point to this at all?
And you sleep.

There is a path, untrod, as yet,
Away from all worry and fret,
An answer I often forget,
While you sleep.

Turn off the light and close the door,
Give up, there's nothing here, I'm sure,
The answer lies across the floor,
Where you sleep.

Simon Baldock